SHERRI HAAB
JEWELRY *inspirations*

SHERRI HAAB
JEWELRY *inspirations*

Techniques and Designs *from* the Artist's Studio

Sherri Haab

WATSON-GUPTILL PUBLICATIONS / NEW YORK

Photos on pages 2, 4, 6, 8, 9, 10 (right), 11, 12, 13, 14, 16, 17, 18, 19, 20, 21, 25 (top left), 30, 34, 38, 44, 49, 52, 53, 54, 58, 61, 62, 65, 71 (bottom), 72, 73, 74, 77, 79 (bottom), 84, 87, 88 (bottom), 91, 95, 104, 105, 106, 114, 116, 120, 134, 135 (bottom), 136, 138, 145 (bottom), 146, 153 (bottom), 157 (bottom left), and 159 © 2009 by Zachary Williams / Williams Visual

All other photos in this book © 2009 by Dan and Sherri Haab

Designer: Kara Plikaitis

First published in the United States in 2009
by Watson-Guptill Publications,
an imprint of the Crown Publishing Group,
a division of Random House, Inc.,
New York

www.crownpublishing.com
www.watsonguptill.com
Library of Congress Cataloging-in-Publication Data
Haab, Sherri.
 Sherri Haab jewelry inspirations : techniques and designs
from the artist's studio / Sherri Haab.
    p. cm.
 Includes index.
 ISBN 978-0-8230-9901-6 (alk. paper)
1. Jewelry making. I. Title.
TT212.H38 2010
739.27--dc22
          2009029413

Printed in China

First printing, 2009

1 2 3 4 5 6 7 8 / 15 14 13 12 11 10 09

Dedicated to my husband, Dan,
who has always encouraged and supported
my artistic endeavors with
patience and love.

ACKNOWLEDGMENTS

Thank you dad, mom, and Laura for providing a wonderful life for me.
Thanks Dan for the technical help and great photos, to Michelle for
how-to photos and styling, to Rachel for design advice and constant
support, and to David for his willingness to jump in and help whenever
needed. Thanks also to Williams Visual Photography, Julie and Marina
Collings, Cheryl Burton, and all of my art colleagues who offered help
with projects. Thank you to all of the manufacturers who supplied
technical help and materials for the projects in the book. And a special
thank you to Joy Aquilino and the staff at Watson-Guptill for their
hard work and enthusiastic support of this project from
conception through to completion.

Contents

Introduction:

    Living a Creative Life   8

In the Studio

DEVELOPING CREATIVITY AND INSPIRATION

A Place of My Own   16
Organized Chaos   16
Looking Back to Think Ahead   19
Creating Idea Notebooks   20
Taking and Teaching Classes   21

JEWELRY-MAKING TECHNIQUES

Basic Wireworking   22
    Tools and Supplies   22
    Working with Jump Rings   23
    Making a Wrapped-Wire Loop   23
    Headpins and Eye Pins   24
Mixing Epoxy Resin Clay   24
Image Transfers   25
2-Part Silicone Mold Putty   26
Mixing Resin   26
Firing Metal Clay   28
Patinas for Metal   29
Knots   30

Memories

Inspiration BY THE SEA   34
Sea Urchin Rings   36
Pacific Ocean Beaded Necklace   38
Sea Glass Image Pendants   42

Inspiration FAMILY HEIRLOOMS   44
Keepsake Photo Necklace   46
Monogram and Silhouette Brass
    Charm Bracelet   49

Seasons

Inspiration HAPPY HALLOWEEN   54
Creepy Creature Papier-Mâché Pins   56
Halloween Button Necklace   58

Inspiration FALL INTO WINTER   62
Polymer Clay Acorn Charms   64
Winter Solstice Charm Exchange Bracelet   68

Collections

Inspiration FAIRY TALES AND FLOWERS   74
Resin Clay Flower Bracelets   76
Fairy-Tale Bubble Necklace   80

Inspiration BEADS, BUTTONS, AND CHARMS   84
Antique Button Pendants   86
Lucite Flower Bracelets   89
Vintage Glass Bead Earrings   92
    Cascading Violet Crystal and Pearl Earrings   94
    Briolette Stone Earrings with Bead Accents   96
    Wrapped-Wire Briolette Bead Earrings   98
Cracker Jack Charm Bracelet   100

Blast from the Past

Inspiration JUST ONE WORD: PLASTICS   106
Rock 'n' Roll Shrink Art Necklaces   108
Resin Heart Pendants   111

Inspiration GETTING GROOVY WITH FIBER   114
Stick-Woven Fiber Bracelet   116
Spool Knit Wire Bracelet   120
Viking Knit Wire Bracelet   126
Braided Handkerchief and Ribbon Bracelet   130
Braided Macramé Ribbon Bracelet   132

Hobbies

Inspiration WHAT'S COOKING?   136
Sweet Treats Polymer Clay Charm Bracelet   138
Metal Clay Cookie Mold Pendant   142

Inspiration GARDENING BOTANICALS   146
Etched Copper Botanical Bracelet   148
Metal Clay Molded Bee Pendant   154

Contributors   158
Resources   158
Index   160

Introduction

My passion in life has always been to create things. I've been making arts and crafts projects ever since I was old enough to hold a pair of scissors or use a bottle of glue. My mother, sister, and grandmother also enjoyed crafting so from an early age I learned how to sew, paint, sculpt, draw, and work with clay and metal. I enjoy combining these skills with inspiration from past experience to create jewelry, which is my favorite form of art since it's wearable. However, I do have a funny admission to make, while I appreciate jewelry I'm guilty of not wearing it very often. I am so busy making new pieces it just gets in the way.

Living a Creative Life

Some say you can tell what you will enjoy as a career if you look back at what you loved to do as a child. This is true in my case. I had many pivotal events and experiences in my young life that shaped my future interest in both crafts and nonfiction writing. I vividly remember the event that inspired my future career as a book writer. In first grade we went to the library for story time, and the librarian read a picture book written by a child author. I had no idea that kids could get published, and I was so excited by this prospect that I couldn't even pay attention to the story itself. As soon as the story was over, I asked the librarian how I would go about writing a book. She responded that it wasn't reasonable to try to publish an actual book and that instead I should submit a picture or poem to a magazine such as *Highlights*. I felt so disappointed and deflated, because I really wanted to write a book. The desire to someday write one never left me.

The next spark that affected my future profoundly was a big assignment given to our class in fifth grade. Each student had to pick a topic to research extensively and write an expert report on it. I chose to write about cacti, probably because I was interested in houseplants at the time. I enjoyed the process immensely. The knowledge I gained from intense research and study gave me a sense of satisfaction I had never felt before. When I look back

on this experience, I can see that this was the moment I realized I liked writing nonfiction.

As much as I enjoyed writing, art was my favorite subject in school. In grade school, Friday was art day, and I always looked forward to it. At one point while working on one of the more exciting projects, I looked around the room and noticed that I was the only student standing up. I later became conscious that getting up out of my seat was a common occurrence and that I had to stand up to make my project so I could work on it from all angles. In high school, I took every art class available, such as calligraphy, painting, ceramics, and photography. I studied art and illustration in college. I didn't complete my degree, as I decided to pursue writing how-to books instead, but I'm glad that I had the opportunity to study under so many talented artists and illustrators. I learned so many skills from them that I use in my work today. I believe basic elements of composition, color theory, and traditional skills are important for any art-based career.

Through the years, much of the training I've acquired for various craft techniques has come by simply "doing." I'm continually making things, sometimes annoying everyone around me with the messes I make. When I was about ten or eleven years old, I

Decorated eggs made by my mother in the 1970s.

Display jewelry pieces to inspire you.

learned how to crochet and sew and started making doll clothes, dresses, and accessories. Ceramic arts and watercolor painting are also interests I've pursued over the years. Some of my fondest memories from growing up are of making things with my mother, sister, and grandmother. We made holiday decorations, baked cookies, and sewed. My sister and I made lots of little things out of clay and bread dough for our dolls. We made an entire dollhouse full of food items and small appliances for a doll set called "The Sunshine Family" that was manufactured in the early 1970s. The set came with a mother, father, and a baby and had instructions that encouraged kids to make accessories for the doll family. These dolls sparked so many little projects that we loved to make.

After spending my entire life making things, I had the desire to teach and write about the things I had learned over the years. Writing a book became a goal, and I launched into research on how to get published. My sister and I decided to collaborate

on a book, and we both worked hard submitting it to various publishers. As any published author knows, getting your first book published is difficult, and we met with resistance. Due to my sister's perseverance and patience we eventually were able to find a publisher who was interested in our ideas. Our first foray into publishing was a polymer clay how-to book for kids. This project allowed my sister and I the chance to combine our acquired craft and writing skills. It launched both of us into careers of writing how-to books for children. After a number of children's books were published, I decided to write a book for adults about metal clay, which was a fairly new material at the time. I was fascinated by silver clay and very excited to be one of the first authors to publish a book on the subject. The book, *The Art of Metal Clay*, was published in 2003 by Watson-Guptill. It was followed by a number of titles on various crafts for both adults and children. The books led to television appearances and DVDs, as well as to teaching opportunities. I now teach internationally at various art retreats and shows. I also give lectures at conferences

You can make personalized jewelry by incorporating family photos.

Plants and flowers are great sources for jewelry inspiration.

on writing and publishing. As I worked on projects for books, I realized that some of the art materials needed for various projects were not readily available, so I decided to remedy this by starting my own line of craft products: Sherri Haab Designs (www.sherrihaab.com). We sell retail and wholesale supplies through our Web store. Most of all I enjoy making jewelry, sharing ideas, and inspiring others to find a passion for a new skill.

After writing numerous books on a wide variety of jewelry-making mediums and techniques, I realized there's a common thread running through my work. Most of my projects are derived from craft ideas, skills, and experiences from my past. At the encouragement of my editor, Joy Aquilino, we decided it was time to share the inspiration behind some of my jewelry designs. Each project in this book has a story behind it and was inspired by something from my past. Some of the projects are based on traditional skills such as needlework or macramé that can be incorporated into jewelry projects. Other designs were inspired

by fond memories, such as the jewelry that incorporates favorite illustrations or family photos.

The fun of making your own jewelry is that it can represent who you are and what you love. In writing this book I chose to include projects using a variety of processes and materials—metal, resin, clay, fiber arts, and glass—so that you will be sure to find something that resonates with you and a project that allows you to tell your own story. Colorful candy-inspired pieces, etched vintage metal, and plenty of image-related pieces are all wonderful ways to make personal statements in your work. This book gives you a little insight into the way I approach jewelry making and what inspires me. Use the techniques and ideas to customize the projects to suit your own memories and lifestyle. Combine techniques to come up with more original ideas based on the skills you already have, and enjoy the process!

In the
Studio

Taking ART CLASSES helps to expand your creativity.

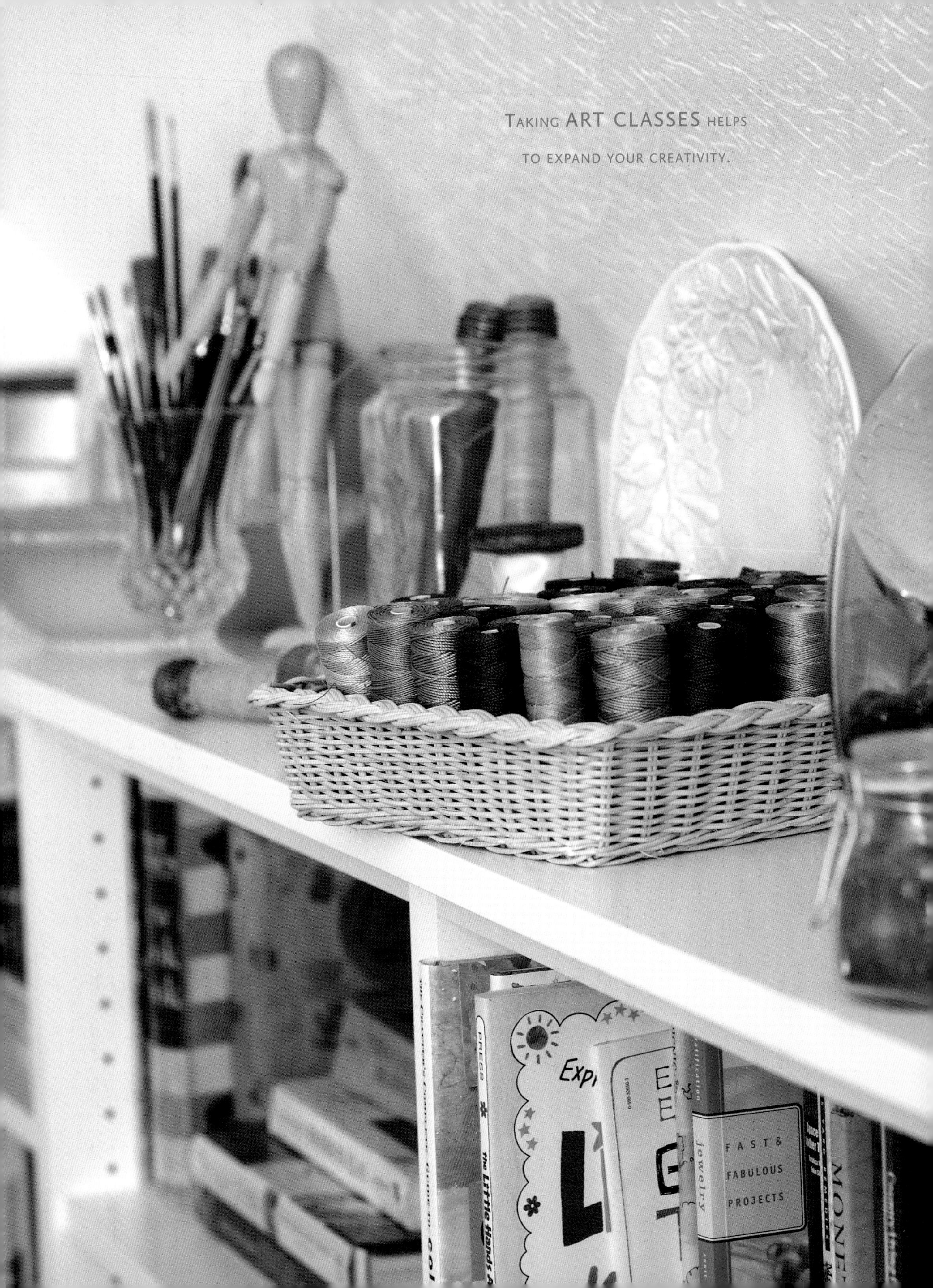

There are a number of ways you can develop your creativity and find inspiration through daily life experiences. By simply having a desire to create, habits of collecting and organizing ideas become second nature. This section gives you insight into how I find inspiration and draw from life experiences to create. By educating myself, collecting ideas, and actively pursuing new skills, I can foster creativity and grow as an artist. The files and ideas collected over the years have become valuable resources. By creating a studio full of cherished supplies that are close at hand, I work freely when I'm busy designing a new project.

Along with having the right environment and resources, there are fundamental skills that are essential to jewelry making. I cover essential techniques for working with a variety of materials, including metal, resin, clay, fiber arts, and glass. I'm sharing my ideas and techniques with you to inspire you to create your own designs based on what's important and close to your heart.

Developing Creativity and Inspiration

The most valuable lesson I've learned about developing creativity has come from observing students I've taught over the years. At many a workshop, distressed students will ask me how to fix a piece that didn't turn out the way they intended. Some are almost in tears as they point out the perceived flaws: "My edges aren't straight," "The color isn't uniform," "My stitches aren't even" — the list goes on and on. They don't see the piece from an outside perspective. Those little, unexpected "flaws" are the magic that makes each piece unique.

I know what you're thinking—it's the same thing that goes through the student's head: "She is just trying to pacify me and make me happy about my disaster." I used to feel the same way about my art and was surprised when others preferred my less-than-perfect pieces. It wasn't until I was the one viewing from the outside perspective that I finally understood why the unintentional is appealing. To my surprise, those student "failures" are ultimately my favorite pieces from the class. I'm not kidding! It's coloring outside the lines; the imperfection, the emotion, and the soul that the cracks reveal. Lost and found edges, asymmetry, and unintentional marks are just a few examples of "mistakes" that actually add to the character and charm of a piece. When we fear that our piece isn't going to turn out perfectly, this holds us back. Creativity is the ability to allow ourselves to be okay with something spontaneous or unintentional. Sometimes this leads us to an inspired direction and to unexpected findings that help us to expand creatively.

Once we are able to be more open and accepting of our own work, inspiration can flow freely. The idea isn't to take everything so seriously but to enjoy the process as much as the end result. A perfect example of a piece I made for this book is the Fairy-Tale Bubble Necklace (see page 80). It's very childlike and features a favorite fairy-tale illustration under a clear dome surrounded by brightly colored clay and rhinestones. The piece is risky because it certainly isn't very sophisticated or "fine," but it's fun. To my surprise this necklace gets more attention than many other pieces I show people. Both of my adult daughters have asked to keep it as soon as I'm ready to give it to one of them. To me this piece represents my love for color and illustration, and my decision to add the clay and sparkly gems reflects crafts I've so enjoyed since childhood. By combining the content with the medium, I'm able to share something through art and bring a smile to someone viewing the piece.

Find a place in your home that is comfortable to create. This is my studio.

Organize and display jewelry pieces to inspire you.

A PLACE OF MY OWN

Creating a studio or work space can be a challenge, especially if you work with a variety of materials. Working in a small space with limited storage can be even more of a challenge. I have a small studio room dedicated to my work, but often my projects drift out into the rest of the house. I've learned over time that the only way to get things done is to let things get messy for a while; and if I have a space where I can leave works in progress, it helps. No matter how little space you have to work with, you can make it your own oasis.

A few musts for the studio are a tabletop that can get banged up a bit, a comfortable chair, and good lighting. Small task lamps make a big difference in the workability of your space. Along with all of the necessary items, it helps to surround your work area with things that inspire you, such as fabric swatches, small pieces of art, jewelry displays, and even music.

ORGANIZED CHAOS

Life is busy. I find it impossible to stay as organized as I would like. I get so excited about new projects that I tend to start ten things at once, underestimating how long it takes to complete each one. Often the minute my feet hit the floor in the morning I dash up to my studio, anxious to get to work. Since I'm more of a night person, the early part of the day is spent on noncreative tasks such as e-mail and business matters. My creativity kicks in later in the afternoon and peaks about 10 PM. I live on chocolate chips and herb tea to keep me going for long hours. Among the candy wrappers, I have to-do lists and Post-it Notes littering my desk. Despite the chaos, I try to run a few miles in the mornings to maintain clarity and balance. I think every creative person has to find what works best for him or her, and how to balance life.

left: Beading supplies for a work in progress.

below: Keep supplies organized for easy access.

above: Keep notes for inspiration in view.

My collection of magazines and reference books.

File folders full of magazine clippings, patterns, notes and ideas, organized by craft medium or topic.

I'm not sure there's a way to ever be totally organized; personally, if I were organized I wouldn't have time to create. I have to work in waves, creating for a deadline and then trying to find time to regroup and reorganize. I have lots of books on organizing, but as one artist friend said, "You need to keep everything out in view to be inspired; if it's put away it's forgotten." What a challenge to those of us who favor a vast array of art materials. I try to at least group things in common so I can find them quickly when working on a project. I have beads arranged by color in small clear jars where I can see them. Tools and findings are organized in shallow drawers or boxes. I have stacks of divided plastic organizers in which I keep small pieces, sorted by metal type or bead color.

LOOKING BACK TO THINK AHEAD

I'm not sure when or why I started collecting craft ideas clipped from magazines, but I have a collection of files dating back to the early '70s. Whenever I found a cool idea in a magazine or came across a pattern I wanted to make someday, I would clip or copy the idea and put it in a portable file box filled with labeled folders. I still keep files today, and attempt to organize them by topic. I like to keep the articles loose because I weed through them from time to time and get rid of some depending on my current interests.

The files are very useful for sparking creativity, as you tend to collect ideas that suit your artistic style and interests. It also saves space to tear out individual articles to file rather than

Keep a sketchbook handy to organize your thoughts and ideas. I made a hand-bound idea book and embellished it with silver and resin; this makes it feel special to me.

My sketches for jewelry designs.

saving the entire magazine. I found that keeping the articles in a scrapbook or ring binder didn't work for me; it took too much time and effort. I admire people who are this organized, but that's not me. My worn files are very functional and serve as a helpful resource for researching timeless techniques.

CREATING IDEA NOTEBOOKS

Many artists keep sketchbooks filled with ideas. I like to keep ideas in a notebook with written descriptions and sketches of ideas for jewelry making. It's nice to take a small sketchbook with you on your travels. Some of the places that might inspire you are museums, galleries, and cultural or historic locations.

It's a good idea to keep a notebook by a bedside table, as many creative ideas pop into your head just before you drift off to sleep or upon waking, when your mind is in a relaxed state. Being creative is an exercise in problem solving. Sleep facilitates insights that often solve a problem; new ideas and designs form through this process. The challenge is trying to capture insights and translate them into finished works. Surrounding yourself with things that inspire you can help this process both in your waking and sleeping hours.

My studio doubles as a classroom, as I teach jewelry-making classes here.

TAKING AND TEACHING CLASSES

Taking a jewelry-making class is a great way to keep you inspired and involved. When looking for a class, you may want to check out local art schools, bead shops, or community programs. I enjoy taking classes and learning from other artists as well as teaching classes myself. I find that as a teacher I often learn even more than the students I'm teaching. We all learn from one another, and working in a group isn't only socially enjoyable, it's a catalyst for getting fired up about new ideas and insights from the people around you. Since most artists work in isolation, it's refreshing to go on retreats, form an art group, or attend a conference.

Jewelry-Making Techniques

This book covers a range of techniques and mediums that are used to create jewelry. Each project was derived from a unique inspiration or theme. The jewelry pieces consist of a collection that uses a variety of materials, including metal, resin, clay, fiber arts, and glass.

Even though each project is very different in style, basic jewelry-making techniques are incorporated throughout, including wirework and beading techniques. Refer to these basic techniques to complete the projects.

BASIC WIREWORKING

One fundamental beading skill you will find helpful is the ability to work with wire. Wire is used to make attachments and to create basic jewelry designs. With the right tools, such as pliers and wire cutters, it's easy to make wrapped loops, bead dangles and to attach clasps. Wire is available in a variety of metals and finishes as well as gauges. Quite a few projects in the book utilize wire in the design. I chose colored enamel wire to match the clay and resin elements for projects such as the Halloween Button Necklace (page 58), Fairy-Tale Bubble Necklace (page 80), and Sweet Treats Polymer Clay Bracelet (page 138). For other projects, such as the Keepsake Photo

Necklace (page 46), oxidized sterling was used to harmonize with the vintage style of the piece. Practice wireworking techniques with inexpensive craft wire and you will quickly find using wire in your work invaluable.

Tools and Supplies

It's important to invest in good tools for jewelry making. Well-made jeweler's pliers make a difference in the quality of your work, and they are easier on your hands in the long run. Just a few basic types are used to complete all of the projects in the book. For the projects in this book, the basic pliers needed are:

Chain-nose pliers. Used to open and close jump rings. Also used to grip or hold wire or to crimp the ends of a wire wrap. These are similar to needle-nose pliers but don't have teeth like needle-nose pliers.

Round-nose pliers. These are an essential tool for forming wire loops. They have a graduated tip for making loops of various sizes.

Wire cutters. A good pair of flush cutters will cut the end of a wire cleanly. A heavy-duty pair of wire cutters from the hardware store are good to have for heavy gauges of wire.

Found objects are combined with beads to make one-of-a-kind jewelry pieces.

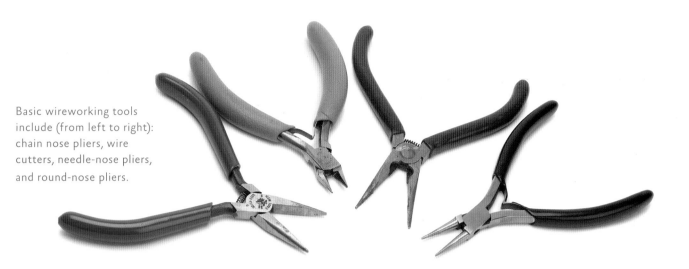

Basic wireworking tools include (from left to right): chain nose pliers, wire cutters, needle-nose pliers, and round-nose pliers.

Working with Jump Rings

Jump rings are round wire rings that can be opened and then closed to make jewelry attachments. They are used to link chain elements together, to attach charms, or to use as part of a clasp. You can buy jump rings in various gauges and diameters, or you can make them by winding wire around a form and then cutting or clipping the wire sections to make individual rings.

To open jump rings you will need two pairs of chain-nose pliers. To open the jump ring, pull one of the pliers toward you and push the other pair away. Don't pull jump rings open and apart; this weakens them by adding stress to the metal. To close the jump ring, bring the wires back to meet in the center in the same fashion as they were opened.

Making a Wrapped-Wire Loop

Wire wrapping is used to secure wire ends either at the base of a loop or along a section of wire to cover it. Wrapped wire is functional as well as decorative.

1. Make a 90-degree bend in the wire. Form a loop with round-nose pliers. Attach the loop to the charm or chain.

2. Hold the loop with chain-nose pliers. Wrap the wire around the base of the loop a few times to secure. Clip off the excess wire with wire cutters and tuck in the end of the wire with chain-nose pliers.

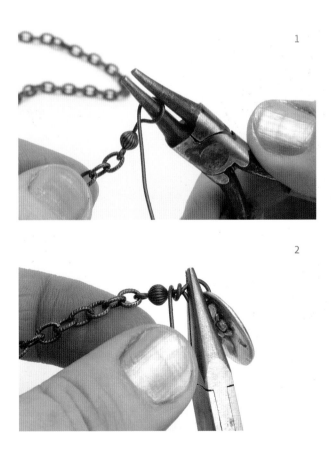

1

2

When opening a jump ring, pull forward with one of the pliers and back with the other; don't pull out to the sides, as that would weaken the ring.

Head Pins and Eye Pins

Head pins are a length of wire with either a flat pad or a decorative ball on one end. They are used to make bead or charm dangles. The pad or ball end acts as a stop to keep the bead from sliding off. I often use these to make decorative attachments, securing them to a piece by making a wrapped loop at the top of the pin to attach and finish it.

Eye pins are similar to head pins except that they have a loop instead of a pad or ball at one end. The loop allows you to link pieces or add bead dangles.

Beads were attached to this head pin and then a loop was formed at the top to attach to the piece. The wire was then wrapped at the base of the loop to secure.

MIXING EPOXY RESIN CLAY

Epoxy resin clay is a 2-part formulation that cures to a durable plastic after it has been mixed. A catalyst mixed with the resin clay causes a chemical reaction, which results in a curing process at room temperature. The clay is precolored and can be mixed to create a variety of custom colors. Mix the custom color of the resin clay before adding the catalyst to make sure the premixed clay and the catalyst are measured and mixed evenly.

The cool thing about epoxy resin clay is that it doesn't require heat to cure, which allows you to embed plastic and other found objects that otherwise wouldn't survive being heated. Because the clay is an epoxy, it also holds the embedded pieces in place without the need to glue them in afterward. The clay is available in a few brands, and is very strong when cured, making it a good choice for jewelry making. Epoxy resin clay is used to make the Sea Urchin Rings (page 36), the Resin Clay Flower Bracelet (page 76), and the Fairy-Tale Bubble Necklace (page 80).

1. Pinch off an equal-sized ball of each component of the epoxy resin clay—the colored clay and the catalyst clay. You can mix your own custom colors prior to adding the catalyst, kneading the colors together before adding an equal amount of the catalyst portion.

2. Knead the colored clay and the catalyst clay well—until the combined clay is a uniform color and thoroughly mixed. The clay has a working time of about 30 minutes to 1 hour; it will become progressively harder as it starts to catalyze. It will take at least overnight for the clay to fully cure. Let it sit on waxed paper as it cures, as it may stain or react with certain surfaces or table finishes.

IMAGE TRANSFERS

ITS™ is a transfer medium that allows you to transfer images onto metal and other nonporous surfaces (such as glass). This product produces soft, transparent images that allow the metal (or other surface) to shine through what used to be the unprinted, or "white," area of the copied image. It gives an ethereal, vintage look to your finished piece. This technique is unique because it allows you to personalize your jewelry with photos or favorite images. The image transfer process is used for the Sea Glass Image Pendants (page 42) Monogram and Silhouette Brass Charm Bracelet (page 49).

1. Print images on ITS paper using a toner-based laser copier. Size the images prior to printing using a computer software program such as Photoshop to fit the shape and size of the surface. If the image has text, make sure to print it as a mirror image, as the text will need to be in reverse so that it will print correctly after the transfer process. Trim the image to fit the surface (metal or glass) exactly when it is placed image side down on the surface. Brush a layer of ITS solution onto the surface; make sure the coating isn't too thin.

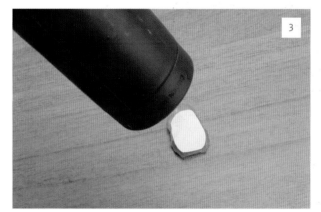

2. Quickly press the image facedown onto the solution. Burnish (make smooth by rubbing) the image to ensure that there are no air bubbles. Wipe away any excess solution around the edge of the paper with a paper towel.

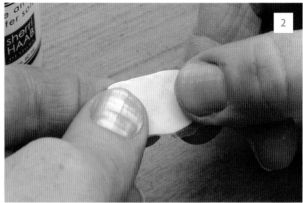

3. Heat set the pieces in a preheated oven set at 325 degrees Fahrenheit for 30 minutes. Or you can use an embossing heat gun tool. Place the pieces on a heatproof surface such as a tile and heat them with the tool for 1 minute.

4. Let the pieces cool completely. To remove the paper, soak the pieces in water for about 10 minutes. Carefully work the paper off, starting from the center out and rolling most of the paper off with your fingernails. If needed, remove the remaining paper, which will appear as a white film on the surface, with 1200 grit wet/dry polishing paper until the image feels perfectly smooth and appears clear.

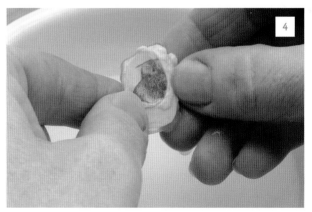

2-Part Silicone Mold Putty

Silicone mold putty is a 2-part putty that becomes a solid rubber material after a catalyst is mixed with the rubber component. The result is a flexible mold for casting clay or interesting resin. It doesn't need a release agent to be used for casting, as the rubber won't stick to most surfaces. You can use this putty to make molds from a variety of small objects. I make molds from antique buttons, collected figurines, seashells, and architectural details. The molds are very useful, as you can use them over and over again, casting a variety of materials from the molds. I cast fine silver charms to replicate old plastic charms for the Cracker Jack Charm Bracelet (page 100) and acorns cast in polymer clay for the Polymer Clay Acorn Charms (page 64) using this versatile material.

1. Knead equal parts of each component of the 2-part silicone mold putty until the putty is uniform in color.

2. Form the putty into a ball and flatten it on a smooth, clean surface. Press the ornament into the putty facedown, making sure the putty surrounds the ornament on all sides.

3. Let the putty set up with the ornament in place. You can tell the putty has cured if you press on it with your fingernail and it bounces back without leaving an impression. This takes about 30 minutes or less. Remove the ornament.

4. Press a ball of soft clay into the mold, smoothing the back of the clay to fill the edge of the mold. Remove excess clay as necessary. Flex the mold to release the clay; the clay should fall out of the mold easily.

Mixing Resin

Resin can be used either as a coating or to make solid cast objects. For coating purposes, resin protects elements in a bezel by adding a "glasslike" coating. It can be poured deeply, allowing you to layer collage elements or small found objects into deep bezels. For casting, you can pour resin into molds, which will become solid. The cast resin pieces can be used to make beads, pendants, and other small objects for jewelry. Resin is used for several projects in the book. Coating resin is used in projects such as the Keepsake Photo Necklace (page 46) and to fill button bezels in the Halloween Button Necklace (page 58). Cast resin is used to make the Resin Heart Pendants (page 111).

One thing to note is that most of the projects in this book use epoxy resin, which is available in various forms and brand names. Each has different characteristics, from thin and thick viscosities to curing times. Quick-setting and gel-type resin epoxies sold in hardware stores are used in some of the projects to attach findings. These are mixed similarly to the pourable types, but due to the thickness and small amount of epoxies, these types are mixed with a toothpick on a piece of waxed paper rather than stirred as liquid in a cup. Both will catalyze when mixed properly and in the right proportions.

Before using resin, follow all manufacturer safety guidelines. Resin can cause dermatitis, so wear gloves if you're worried about touching it. Resin should be handled with care, and you should avoid getting it on your skin. You should also use eye protection and wear a respirator fitted with fume filters to ensure safety, especially when working with large quantities.

Some types of polyurethane resin are similar to epoxy resin in that they can be mixed 1:1. One of the main differences is that they cure faster. Polyurethane resin is a good resin to use for casting larger pieces, such as the Resin Heart Pendants (page 111).

Accurate measuring and mixing is critical for resin to cure properly. In regard to measuring, the resins used in the projects in this book were chosen because they can be measured easily by volume (1:1 ratio). The resin was measured by pouring each component into graduated mixing cups, and carefully filling according to the markings on the cup indicated for ounces, teaspoons, or cubic centimeters.

To mix resin with hardener, measure the resin component into a plastic measuring cup and then measure an equal amount of hardener. Most manufacturers recommend that you avoid mixing small amounts (less than ¼ ounce of each component) to ensure success. Stir the resin well to incorporate the resin and hardener.

Stir, scraping the sides without whipping, as whipping or folding will cause more air bubbles to form. After mixing the resin, pour the mixture into a clean cup and mix again briefly. Transferring the resin into a second cup, and the second stirring will ensure that the resin is completely incorporated with the hardener and will properly cure without tackiness later. A word of caution: Always mix the proper ratios recommended to avoid overheating which causes the resin to pop or splat.

After pouring the resin into a mold or bezel, remove the air bubbles with a heat-embossing gun. These are commonly found in craft stores with the rubber stamp supplies. Hold the heat gun directly overhead (holding the heat gun at an angle will cause the resin to spill over); the heat will remove most of the bubbles.

Let the resin cure in a warm place for at least 72 hours. The warmth of a lightbulb is ideal for curing resin. Test the resin by tapping it with a toothpick; it should feel hard like glass if cured properly.

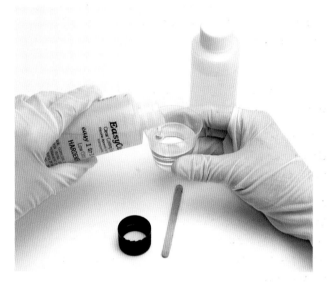

Measure your resin and hardener accurately.

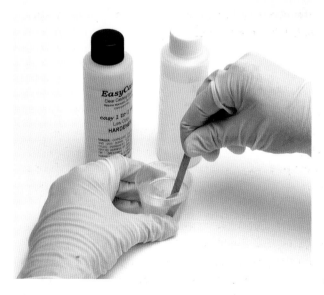

Stir the resin well to ensure that it catalyzes properly.

FIRING METAL CLAY

Metal clay consists of microscopic metal particles suspended in a mixture of an organic binder and water. The clay looks very much like modeling clay. It's smooth and pliable and can be worked with your hands. According to the manufacturer, metal clay is nontoxic and safe to use. It can be textured, rolled, carved, or sculpted to make jewelry, beads, vessels, and small sculptures. Once a metal clay object is fired, the binder burns away and the metal particles sinter, or fuse together. The final product emerges as a metal piece that can be marked as such.

In the late 1990s I discovered this amazing material. At the time the material was so new that there were very few sources of information about how to use it. I took classes from some well-known metalsmiths, including Tim McCreight. It wasn't long before I decided to write a book on metal clay: *The Art of Metal Clay*. It was one of the first mass-market books on the subject. Metal clay continues to be one of my favorite jewelry-making mediums.

Metal clay must be fired at high temperatures in order to sinter properly. Low-fire types of metal clay can be fired with a small handheld torch instead of in a kiln. This is the same type of torch used to caramelize sugar for crème brûlée. Butane fuel for the torch—the same fuel that's used to fill cigarette lighters—is available at grocery and variety stores. Torch firing works for small pieces (smaller than a silver dollar and/or projects made with less than 25 grams of metal clay). Low-fire silver clay was used for the projects in this book because it can be torch fired quite successfully. To fire metal clay with a torch, follow these steps:

Butane Torch-Firing Instructions for Metal Clay

1. Make sure your piece is completely dry. Place the dried metal clay piece on a firebrick or solderite pad. Make sure you're working on a heat-proof table and away from anything combustible.

2. Fill the torch with butane. Ignite the torch and hold it over the piece at a very close range—about 1½ inches away.

3. Move the torch slowly over the piece. A small flame and smoke will appear briefly as the binder burns out.

4. Keep the torch moving and watch as the piece glows red-orange. It's easier to see the orange color in a darker room, away from bright light or sunlight. Keep the metal glowing with even heat for proper fusing, and at the same time avoid melting the piece, which can happen quickly if you're not paying attention.

5. As soon as the piece begins to glow red-orange, start timing. Fire for at least 2 minutes for a small piece. Large pieces can take a few minutes longer—up to 5 minutes. These are minimum times; it doesn't hurt to fire any piece longer. Keep the piece glowing red-orange the whole time, all the while moving the torch evenly over it. If the piece starts to shimmer or looks shiny, that means the silver is beginning to melt. Quickly pull the torch back. Continue firing, adjusting the torch distance as needed. After firing, turn off the torch and let the piece air cool.

6. After firing and cooling the piece, use a brass brush and burnishing tools to bring up the shine of the silver to finish.

Small, handheld torch and butane fuel.

Low-fire silver metal clay can be fired with a butane torch.

PATINAS FOR METAL

To add an aged or vintage look to metal, patinas are applied to oxidize certain metals. If you're working with vintage pieces, often you want the findings and wire elements to match, so patina solutions come in handy for this purpose. I use patinas to bring out details in richly textured pieces. I used two common patina solutions to darken silver and copper throughout the projects that use these metals in the book.

Patina solutions, which are available through jewelry suppliers, add color or darken the metal through the process of oxidation. They are corrosive in nature, so be sure to follow safety precautions, work in a well-ventilated area, and wear gloves and protective gear to protect your skin and eyes. Oxidizing chemicals should be kept away from eating areas and disposed of after use. Check with local authorities about proper disposal methods in your area. Liver of Sulfur and Black Max™ are common patina solutions for metal. The following methods describe how to use each chemical.

Liver of Sulfur is available in solid or liquid form. To begin the patina process using solid chips, dissolve a small chip of dry Liver of Sulfur in hot water. Heat the metal piece by running it under hot water first. Use a wire to dip the piece into the solution and watch as the color moves from golden yellow to blue and finally to blue-black. Remove the piece from the solution when you like the color. Rinse the metal under cold water and dry the piece. Polish with fine sandpapers or buffing pads to remove the patina from the raised areas.

Black Max is an oxidizing solution containing hydrochloric acid. It turns silver or copper black. Apply it to the metal with a cotton swab. Let the piece dry and then buff the raised areas with a polishing pad to remove the patina, leaving it in the recessed areas of the metal.

Another method of adding patina to metal such as copper is by using heat. A small butane torch maybe used to heat the surface of the metal, which will create a patina. This method is used on the Viking Knit Wire Bracelet (page 126).

Mix a small chip of Liver of Sulfur with hot water in a disposable cup to dissolve.

Use a wire to dip a silver charm into the Liver of Sulfur. Remove the piece when the desired color is obtained.

Buff the chain with a polishing pad after the patina dries.

Knots

Knots are used in some of the projects in the book. Macramé knots are used for the braided cord on the Sea Glass Image Pendants (on page 42). Knots are also featured in the Braided and Macramé Fabric Bracelets (on pages 130-134) they use non-traditional materials such as lace and fabric for a softer look. Below are descriptions on how to make these common knots.

Overhand Knot

To tie the knot, make a loop with the cord, bring the end of the cord through the loop, and pull tight. See image 1.

Square Knot

The square knot consists of two opposite half-knots. To tie a half-knot, bring the left cord over the two center (core or filler) cords, like an L shape. Bring the right cord over the tail of the left cord, then under the two middle cords and up through the left loop as shown. Pull the knot tightly against the middle cords to secure.

After tying the first half-knot, tie a second half-knot directly under it. However, the difference is that this second knot is tied starting on the right side, as a mirror of the first knot. It's helpful to practice this knot with two colors of cord to visualize the over-and-under path.

To tie a square knot with just two cords, it's: right over left and then left over right.
See image 2.

Lark's Head Knot

This knot is used to attach cord to a pendant. To tie this knot, fold a cord in half; bring the loop (where you folded the cord in half) up through the hole of the pendant. Bring the ends of the cord through the loop, pulling snugly to cinch up the knot. See image 3.

Braid

Work with three strands of cord, and bring the left strand over the center strand. This cord now becomes the center. Bring the right cord over the center, and now this cord becomes the center and so forth. Follow the pattern, repeating left and right, to form a braid. See image 4.

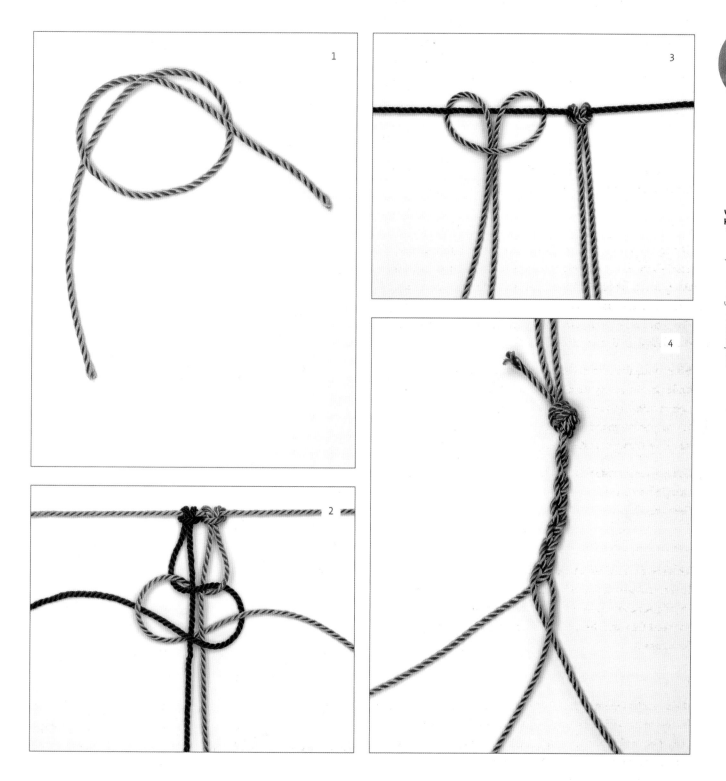

Memories

Sherri (left) and her sister Laura, 1969.

14. Grand Fir

Abies grandis (Dougl.) Lindl.

Grand fir, also commonly called lowland white fir or simply white fir, is probably the most common of the true firs in Washington.

It is used to some extent for timber and pulpwood, and in some sections Christmas trees of grand fir are popular. Demand for lumber during the war put more of this species on the market than ever before.

... twigs, ¾ to 2¼ inches long, usually in ... of the twigs, dark green, marked on the ... bands of stomata.

... low-brown, about ¼ inch long, usually ... slightly hairy at first.

... on young stems, becoming deeply divided into flat ridges. Resin blisters are present on smooth bark. It it purplish-brown in cross-section.

FRUIT is an upright, cylindrical cone, 2 to 4½ inches long, greenish-purple. Cone scales fall off at maturity.

WOOD is pale brown, soft, and light.

IT IS a large tree, 140 to 170 feet tall, 2 to 4 feet in diameter and grows on better sites, forming a rounded head.

15. Noble Fir

Abies procera R...

Noble fir, given the name of larch by loggers ... largest of our true fir ... duces the best timber ... for interior finish and ... eral lumber purposes. ... is largely a mountain ... curring at elevations of ... 3,000 feet ...

LEAVES are scattered s... mostly arranged ... sides, and pointed

BUDS are oblong, blun...

TWIGS are slender, dar...

BARK is dark gray, smo... rect angular plates

FRUIT is an upright, c... which are longer ... pletely enclose th...

WOOD is reddish-brown ...

IT IS a large tree, 160 ... a rather broad, ro...

Engelmann Spruce

...gelmannii Parry

... is slow-growing and ... found m... its ma... a small... wood. Crushed foliage ... disagreeable odor.

... ar species, western white ... grows in ... ains. Its b... cone scales en... ... ns, and needles s... ... inch long.

LEAVES are scattered singly, stand out from all sides of the twigs, four-sided, 1 to 1⅛ inches long, blue-green, with pointed tips and

Quaking Aspen

Populus tremuloides.

Some authors list ... *tremuloides aurea* Dan... variety, *P. tremuloi...* Sarg. grows on ... Sound. Its ... at first, la... and rough... ...d or h... ...te-serrate ... ...wever, ar... ...aluable here ... ...gton, aspen is ... ...alleys and on nort...

LEAVES are alternate,

Inspiration BY THE SEA

I grew up in the Pacific Northwest, near Seattle, Washington. My father has a great respect for nature, so our family spent many weekends exploring the local forests and beaches. I was intrigued by sea life, especially the treasures to be found in the sand (which in that area was actually more like fine rocks). The shores were lined with sea cucumbers, crabs, mussels, and various seaweeds. When I was very young, I found a strand of bullwhip kelp. I was so enamored by it that I carried it around our campsite for several days until it started to smell and then my parents made me get rid of it.

The dark, overcast days so common in the Northwest never fazed me as a child. My friends and I played outdoors for hours down by the creek in our neighborhood park. I have vivid memories of examining its plant life, bugs and other creatures (including slugs—yuk!) and whatever else lived on its mossy banks. In our own backyard, I have memories of my dad making a whistle from an alder tree branch in the spring when the bark was green—just perfect for making slide whistles. It was amazing to me that you could make a working whistle with just a knife and a branch.

Those memories have a strong impact on my jewelry designs. Ferns, dogwoods, starfish, wildflowers, pinecones, gray rocks, and birds are all themes I love to explore, because they remind me of the natural surroundings of my childhood.

Sea Urchin Rings

My dad always called my sister and me "urchins" (he used this as a term of affection). These Sea Urchin Rings were inspired by the beautiful spiny creatures you will find in the waters and tide pools along the Pacific Northwest coast. They are found in nature in a variety of beautiful colors. You can replicate the colors using beads and sequins in coral red, blue-green, or violet, mixing the clay to match your beads of choice.

SUPPLIES

Apoxie® Sculpt 2-part epoxy resin clay (*Aves® Studio*)

Seed beads

Sequins

Head pins

Wire clippers

Ring blank with 12mm pad
(*Sherri Haab Designs*)

320 or 400 grit sandpaper

2-part quick-setting epoxy resin

Toothpicks

Waxed paper

1. Pinch off a small ball of epoxy resin clay and catalyst. Make sure each ball of clay and catalyst is equal in size. Mix the two components thoroughly until uniform in color (see directions on page 24). Form the ball of clay into a small mound. Slide a bead and a sequin onto a head pin that has been clipped to a short length. It's helpful to prepare several head pins prior to starting the project so they will be ready to use. This will give you time to insert them before the clay starts to cure. Push the head pin into the clay.

2. Continue to push head pins into the clay in the same fashion until the mound is covered. (Think of covering a pincushion.)

3. Let the clay cure overnight. To attach the finished piece to a ring blank, sand the pad with 320 or 400 grit sandpaper prior to attaching the clay dome so the clay will adhere better. Mix the 2-part epoxy resin with a toothpick on waxed paper (see directions on page 26–27).

4. Apply a small amount of the epoxy resin to the sanded pad of the ring blank and attach the clay dome. Prop up the ring so it sits level as it cures, and let it set overnight until cured.

5. Check all of the head pins to make sure they are secure in the clay, and use the epoxy resin to fasten any of them that are loose.

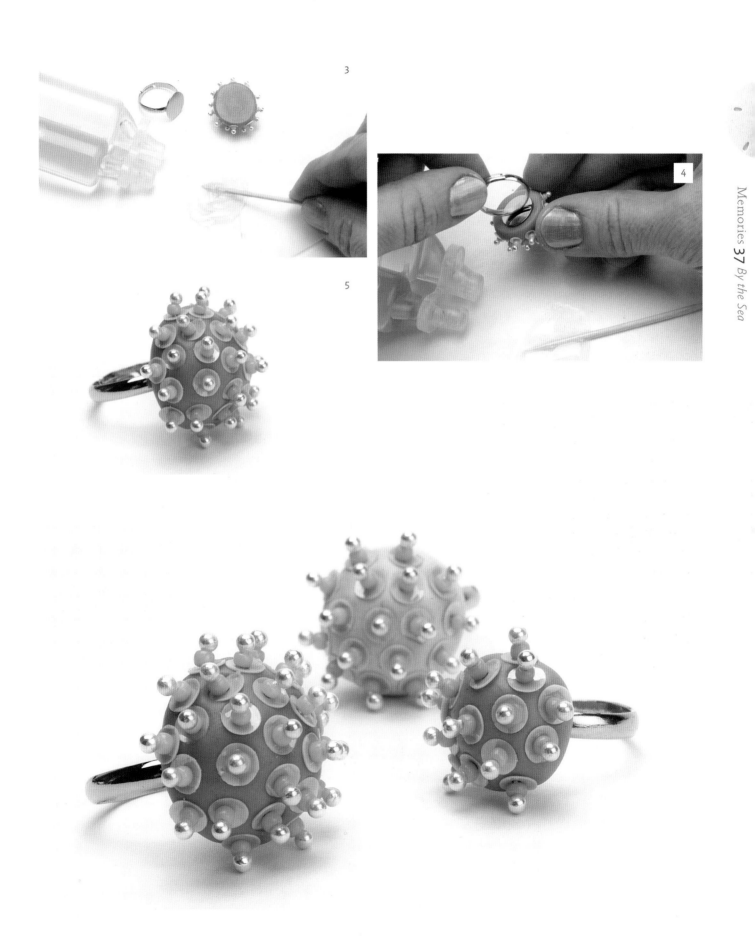

Pacific Ocean Beaded Necklace

The combination of Labradorite stones and gray-colored pearls reminds me of the colors and organic shapes you will find on the rocky beaches of the Pacific Northwest. This multistrand necklace is made using carded silk cord with a beading needle attached. You can use synthetic cord if you prefer and beads in your favorite colors to make variations of this same design.

SUPPLIES

Bead board (*optional*)

Pearls, Labradorite stones, and glass beads

2 cards of Griffin silk cord (*2 meters each*) with beading needle attached, size 2 or 3, or synthetic cord

2-inch piece of medium- or large-diameter French wire (*also known as bullion*) (*must fit over 2 pieces of the silk cord*)

Wire cutters

Loop-and-toggle clasp

Scissors

Pointed tweezers

Ruler

G-S Hypo Cement

1. Use a bead board if you have one to organize the arrangement of pearls and stone beads for the design, spacing them as desired for an 18-inch necklace. Unwind and dampen the bead cord with water to remove the folds in the cord before beginning.

2. To start the end of the necklace with a clasp, clip off about a 3/8-inch section of bullion.

3. Slide your first bead onto the cord followed by the bullion piece. Slide the pieces down to the end of the cord until they are about 5 inches from the end. Add the toggle end of the clasp next. Run the needle end of the cord back down through the bead, cinching the bullion up to hold the clasp, leaving a tail end of cord about 3 inches long. Make an overhand knot (see pages 30–31) under the bead to hold it in place.

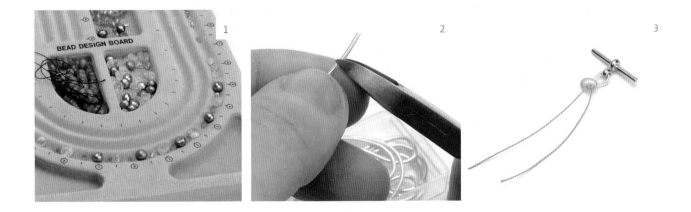

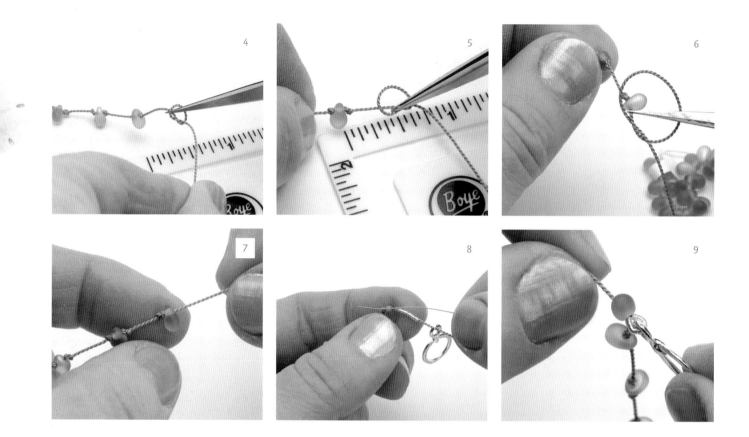

4. The beads and stones will be strung along the cord, spaced equally apart with a single overhand knot on both sides of each bead. After placing a bead, you will measure the distance to place your next bead.

5. Once you have measured from the first bead, tie an overhand knot, but do not pull the knot tight until you use tweezers to guide the placement of the knot. Before tightening the knot, insert the tip of the tweezers inside the loop to hold the cord where the knot will be made. Pull the knot tight and remove the tweezers when the knot is complete.

6. Slide a bead up to the knot. Tie an overhand knot next to the bead, holding the cord inside the loop with tweezers as you pull the knot. The tweezers will keep the knot close to the bead where it needs to be.

7. Once you have added enough beads and stones along the cord to finish the length of the necklace, tie a knot to mark the end or stopping place where the clasp will go. Slide a bead up to the knot without knotting on the other side of the bead.

8. To start the next strand, cut a piece of bullion as you did in step 2. Slide it over the cord and then add the loop end of the clasp. Bring the needle back through the bead.

9. Pull the cord to cinch up the bullion around the clasp and tie an overhand knot under the bead to hold. Continue tying knots and adding beads along the second strand. You can make this strand the same length or slightly longer than the first strand if you want the strands to be graduated in length.

10. As you reach the end of the length of the second strand, you will need to add a new cord if you want to add a third strand. Thread a bead and a new piece of bullion onto the end of the second strand, and thread a new cord up through both the bead and the bullion, leaving a 3-inch cord tail on the end of the new cord.

11. Bring both needles on the cords through the clasp, pulling the bullion around the clasp. Now you will have two bullion loops on the clasp. Bring both cords back through the bead and knot them both under the bead. Clip off the end of the old cord that was used for the two previous strands. Continue tying knots with the new cord to finish the third strand of beads. Make it the same length or graduated in length to complement the other two strands.

12. Add a knot and your last bead followed by a cut piece of bullion. Bring the cord through the clasp and back through the bead. Tie a knot under the bead followed by another finishing knot over the cord for extra security as shown. Clip off loose ends of cord and use jewelry cement to keep the knots from fraying.

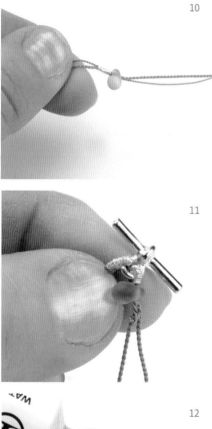

10

11

12

Sea Glass Image Pendants

I spent a lot of time as a child collecting rocks and shells from the beach. Agates are commonly found on Pacific Northwest beaches, and my dad used to show me how they light up if you bang them together. Sea glass has the same beautiful, frosted, translucent look as agates and it's often hard to tell them apart. I love the memories associated with collecting sea glass and agates we scavenged along the shore.

When you look for sea glass, look for pieces with flat surfaces and few imperfections, as they will work best for this project. You can also buy mechanically tumbled glass instead of naturally found sea glass.

SUPPLIES

Laser-printed images on ITS paper
ITS solution
Sea glass (*West Coast Sea Glass*)
1200 grit 3M wet/dry polishing paper
Wood block
Pan
Water

Dremel drill or flex-shaft tool
Diamond-coated drill bits, 1.5–2mm twist type
Renaissance wax or ITS sealer (*Sherri Haab Designs*)
Buffing cloth or old T-shirt
Brush
C-Lon® bead cord

Scissors
Cord crimp clasp
Chain-nose pliers
G-S Hypo Cement

Optional
Beading needle
Beads

TIP: You can drill holes in the glass pieces before applying the images instead of after they are applied if you prefer.

1. Select your image and transfer it to the sea glass (see directions on page 25). To drill a hole in the top of the glass, place it on a wood block in a pan of water. There should be enough water so that the glass is covered and is just below the surface of the water. Use a small, diamond-coated drill bit to begin drilling the hole. Hold the piece firmly on the wood as you drill and nick the glass to make an initial pilot mark by holding the drill at an angle.

2. Bring the drill upright steadily on that mark until the drill is perpendicular to the glass. Let the drill bit continue to drill under water without putting pressure on the bit. Simply hold the drill steady and let the weight of the drill provide the pressure. Depending on the glass it may take about 10–15 minutes for the drill to go through it, be patient as the drill works. When you feel the drill break through to the wood block you will know the hole is done. If you want the hole to be larger work progressively up in size with another bit or two until the hole is the right size.

3. After drying off the piece, seal the image with a layer of wax or ITS sealer. If you're using wax, use a small, fingertip amount of it and buff with a buffing cloth or an old T-shirt to add sheen. If you're using the ITS sealer, brush on one coat, let it dry for 30 minutes, and then bake for 30 minutes at 325 degrees Fahrenheit to cure.

4. To attach the pendant to the cord, start by cutting three strands of cord, each about 1 yard in length. Bundle the cords together and fold them in half to form a loop. Push this loop of cords down through the hole in the sea glass pendant. Bring the six loose ends through this loop and pull, forming a lark's head knot (see directions on pages 30–31). Braid the three cords on each side. To add beads to the braid, use a beading needle to sew beads along the braid, passing the needle in and out along the woven pattern of the braid and threading on a bead as desired.

5. Add a cord crimp clasp finding with chain-nose pliers. Knot and off cut the ends, finishing with a bit of jewelry glue over the cut ends of the cord to prevent fraying.

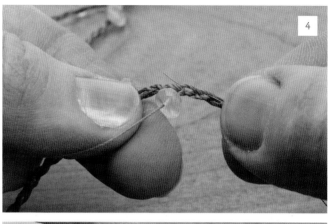

Mr & Mrs R.L. Hofm
+
family

The Post-Register, Idaho Falls, Idaho

SUGAR BEET CHAMPIONS DRAW SALUTE

FIVE YEAR DIARY

PRESS

KID RADIO AND TELEVISION
IDAHO FALLS, IDAHO

WILL APPRECIATE YOUR GRANTING ALL
COURTESIES EXTENDED TO PRESS AND
RADIO TO JIM HOFFMAN

AN OFFICIAL KID NEWS
REPORTER

Approved by _____

HAILED AS East Idaho's sugar beet growing champions this week were Shirley Gray, above, 4-H club member from Bonneville County, and arry Christensen, second from right, Future Farmer chapter member from Firth, They, along th county winners in both 4-H club and FFA visions, were honored at an awards banquet

the Utah-Idaho Sugar Co. and the Idaho First National Bank. Keith Ellis, field specialist for the sugar company, is pictured at left, and Burl Bandell, assistant cashier of the bank, is shown at right, shortly after the two district champions were presented with their $ cash awards.

ASSORTMENT OF 3 Gr. TIMING WASH
FOR SWISS WATCHES BRACELETS

NEWALL

BOT.		RATING		BOT.		
1	6	1 min. in		7		
2		2		8		
3		3		10		
4	9			11		
5	9			12		

No 344 NEWALL Co,
Order refills by size and rating value.

Inspiration FAMILY HEIRLOOMS

In recent years, scrapbooking has become a popular way to preserve family history by combining photos and personal memorabilia with various art techniques and materials, mostly in paper form. For many people, myself included, there's a satisfaction that comes with using personal items such as photos or long-forgotten pages from a recipe book or diary to create a piece of art. It's a wonderful way to appreciate the past in a new light; but I prefer to preserve my family photos, memories, and heirlooms by creating jewelry rather than scrapbook pages. Fabric from my mother's apron, a handwritten note, photos of ancestors, and illustrations from old books often end up as the subjects for the jewelry I make.

Almost anything saved from the past can inspire a jewelry piece. Make color copies of photos or old documents rather than use the originals for your designs. Use beads from a broken piece of jewelry, or include small dimensional items such as a button or a baby bracelet. You might also use a fabric motif or color scheme to inspire a design based on your family history.

Wire wrapping and beaded necklace designs by Cheryl Tempest Burton; bezels by Sherri Haab.

Keepsake Photo Necklace

This is a favorite project of mine for making family gifts. It's a way I can use personal photos in my art. I create charms featuring photos of loved ones for birthdays, weddings, or other special events.

This project features photos that have been reduced in size on a copier to fit in tiny bezels. Black-and-white photos were used in these examples, but color ones would work equally well. Use a photo-editing computer software program such as Photoshop to resize the photos prior to printing or reduce them directly with a copier. Resin protects the images with a durable, glasslike coating. Cheryl Tempest Burton is a mixed-media artist who designed the necklaces for these bezels. She skillfully combines old jewelry parts, sterling silver wire, and vintage beads to create the finished designs.

SUPPLIES

Copied images of photographs,
   black-and-white or color
Scissors
Pewter bezels
   (*Sherri Haab Designs*)
Flat brush
Mod Podge® decoupage medium
   (*Plaid Creative Group*)
Waxed paper

Toothpicks
2-part epoxy resin
Graduated mixing cups
Stir stick
Heat gun
Pieces of chain and broken
   jewelry parts
24-gauge half-hard sterling
   silver wire

Wire cutters
Hammer
Metal block
Bead dangles and accent beads
   (*optional*)
Head pins
Round-nose pliers
2 chain-nose pliers
Clasp

1. Copy and resize photographs to fit the bezel using a photo-editing computer software program such as Photoshop. To cut the photo to fit the bezel, press around the edges of the paper with your fingers to emboss the paper with the edge of the bezel.

2. Cut around this embossed line and check the fit of the paper for the bezel. Trim the paper a little more if necessary until the image fits.

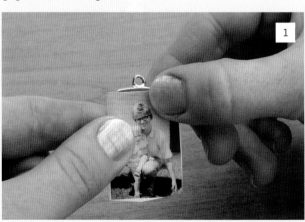

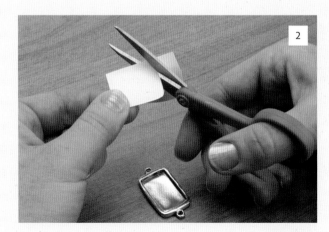

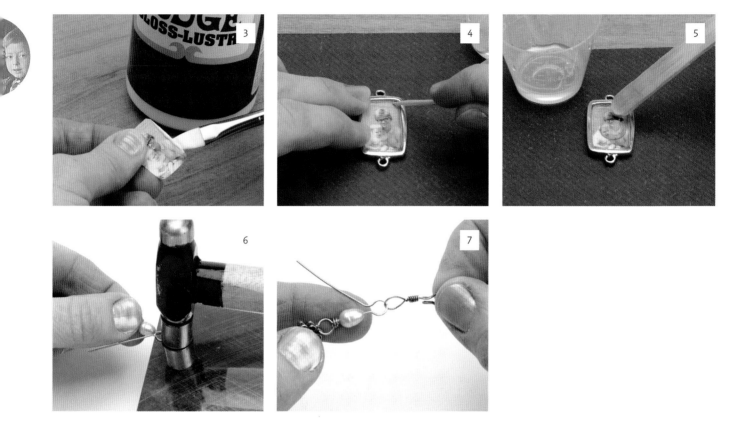

3. To seal, coat the back, front, and edge of the paper with Mod Podge using a flat brush. If the paper isn't properly sealed, the resin will stain the paper. Work on waxed paper to keep the paper from sticking to your work surface as you coat the paper. Let the paper dry thoroughly.

4. Press the image into the bezel. Use a toothpick to tuck the paper in around the inside of the bezel wall. Make sure there are no air bubbles under the paper.

5. Mix the 2-part epoxy resin in a mixing cup (see directions on pages 26–27). Use a wood stir stick to layer the epoxy resin over the image in the bezel, filling the bezel to the top. Use a rubber stamp embossing heat gun to remove any bubbles in the resin. Do not use an

industrial one, as it will be too hot. Let the resin cure in a warm place overnight or until no longer tacky.

6. After the epoxy resin is cured, attach the bezel to chain links and segments of old jewelry pieces using wire-wrapping techniques (see directions on pages 22–23). Make wrapped-wire loops to connect the pieces. Flatten some of the loops with a hammer on a metal block to harden them (this will help the loops to maintain their shape).

7. Using round and needle-nose pliers add beads and dangles to embellish the necklace. Add a handmade or purchased wire clasp to finish the necklace.

Monogram and Silhouette
Brass Charm Bracelet

Silhouettes were popular in the past and were often hung on parlor walls with the family portraits. I remember sitting perfectly still as my mother traced my profile onto black paper one sunny day when I was about five. She traced my shadow, which was cast on our back door. Then she cut the tracing out and framed it for hanging. I used this same technique, using a lightbulb rather than the sun to trace the profiles of my family members, to make these silhouette charms.

You might try graphic designs such as a tree, bird, or monogram rather than human forms. Black-and-white clip art is readily available both online and in books. Monograms are nice to use to represent a family name or individual. Use decorative fonts to create letters to transfer. Remember to print them in reverse so they will appear correctly after being transferred.

Monogram and Silhouette Bronze Charm Bracelet

SUPPLIES

Black-and-white silhouette or
  monogram printed on ITS paper
ITS solution
Brass stamping
400 and 600 grit sandpaper
Rubbing alcohol

Cotton swab
1200 grit 3M wet/dry polishing
  paper
Renaissance wax or ITS sealer
  (*Sherri Haab Designs*)
Buffing cloth or old T-shirt

Brush
Charm bracelet chain with
  jump rings
Beads
Head pins
2 chain-nose pliers

1. Select your image and transfer it to the brass stamping (see directions on page 25).

2. Seal the image with a layer of wax or ITS sealer. If you use wax, use a small fingertip amount of it and buff with a buffing cloth or an old T-shirt to add sheen. If you use ITS sealer, brush on one coat, let it dry for 30 minutes, and then bake for 30 minutes at 325 degrees Fahrenheit to cure.

3. Using chain-nose pliers, attach the brass stampings to a purchased charm bracelet chain with jump rings. Add beads and other charms with head pins to embellish the bracelet. (see directions on pages 22–24).

HOW TO MAKE A SILHOUETTE

Tape a piece of black paper to a wall to trace the silhouette. Seat your subject close to the wall and parallel to it so you can view his or her profile. Shine a light on the subject. This will cast a shadow of the profile on the wall. Hold the light farther away to make the shadow smaller or closer to make it larger. Use a pencil to trace the shadow of the profile to create the silhouette. Cut out the silhouette and place the paper on a scanner to copy. Use a photo-editing computer software program such as Photoshop to reduce it to the desired size to fit your metal piece, or have it reduced at your local copy center. In either case, when you're ready to make the transfers, copy the image onto ITS paper using a black-and-white toner copy. If you don't have black paper, trace the silhouette on white paper and then create a black silhouette using a computer software program such as Photoshop or Illustrator.

Seasons

Inspiration HAPPY HALLOWEEN

Halloween is my favorite holiday, but not for the reasons you might think. I don't like to dress up in costumes or play tricks on people, although a good scare can be therapeutic every once in a while. I say this from experience, as from time to time my husband takes great delight in jumping out from behind a corner to surprise me. Hearing his laugh makes it worthwhile.

If you stop to think about it, Halloween is kind of strange, with kids going door-to-door dressed up and begging for candy. But it's great, and one of those rare times when you actually get to see your neighbors. There's a sense of excitement in the air as parents and children get ready to go out for the evening. And then, let's face it, there's candy—lots and lots of it. I have an incurable sweet tooth, so this holiday enables my addiction. I think Halloween candy is the best—the mini-sized candy bars don't count as calories in my book. I also love this time of year, with the fall colors and anticipation of the upcoming holiday season. Halloween decorations are intriguing. There are more than a few talented artists and collectors alike who share a serious passion for this holiday. Some of my favorite picture books and animated films have Halloween themes. Tim Burton, Lane Smith, and Edward Gorey are some of the artists who have influenced me with their quirky, dark, and original interpretations of this holiday.

Creepy Creature Papier-Mâché Pins

Papier-mâché is the perfect medium for sculpting Halloween figures because of its rustic quality. Exaggerate the proportions and features to give the figures character and charm. To make the figures appear to be aged, brush or rub an antiquing gel over the dried paint. My favorite collectibles are paper candy containers from the 1920s. These figures were inspired by the illustration style that was so popular during that period.

SUPPLIES

Creative Paperclay® or CelluClay®
    air-dry paper clay
Sculpting tools
Water

Toothpick
Gesso
Acrylic paints, black, white, orange,
    violet, green

Small brush
Acrylic spray or brush-on sealer
2-part quick-setting epoxy resin
Waxed paper
Pin back finding

1. Pinch off a small amount of the clay to form the figure, keeping the rest of the clay wrapped, as it dries quickly. Sculpt the figure using your hands or sculpting tools as needed. Halloween figures can be rough and asymmetrical.

2. Attach pieces of clay, such as the head, with water. Use a sculpting tool to blend the pieces together at the seams.

3. Water can be used to smooth the clay and to add moisture as needed. Use a sculpting tool or toothpick to form the eyes and mouth. Let the clay figure dry thoroughly according to package directions.

4. Paint the figure with a base coat of gesso.

5. Paint the figure with acrylic paints.

6. Use a small brush for painting details. After the paint dries, protect it with acrylic sealer.

7. Mix the quick-setting epoxy resin with a toothpick on waxed paper. This will be used to attach a pin back.

8. Apply a small amount of the epoxy resin to the back of the figure and press the pin back in place. Let the resin cure overnight.

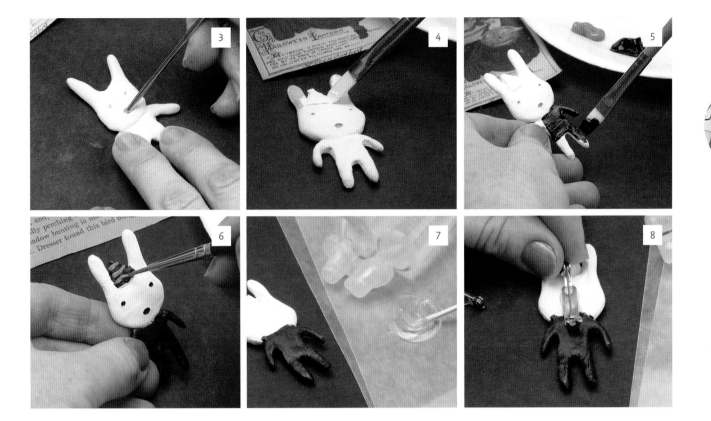

Halloween Button Necklace

Vintage Halloween illustrations are the inspiration for this project. I remember making paper decorations to hang in the windows for Halloween when I was still in grade school. Now I collect vintage postcards, paper decorations, and greeting cards, which remind me of those earlier years. Though highly collectible, you can still find old postcards, candy bags, and crepe paper decorations from antique dealers or auctions. Clip art collections of images are also available from companies such as Dover Publications.

SUPPLIES

Vintage buttons (*recessed with rim that is appropriate for a bezel setting*)

Drill, drill press, or quick-setting epoxy resin, 320 grit sandpaper or any that will rough up the surface, and bail finding

Copied images

Scissors

Mod Podge decoupage medium (*Plaid Creative Group*)

Flat brush

Waxed paper

Chip board (*thin cardboard such as a cereal box*)

ICE Doming Resin™ (*Objects and Elements*)

Graduated mixing cup

Stir stick

Needle-nose pliers or wire cutters

Chain

Beads

Plastic-coated wire-black or head pins

Round-nose pliers

2 chain-nose pliers

Jump ring

Clasp

1. Choose buttons with an edge or rim that will serve as a bezel setting for the images. Drill a hole in the top of the button for hanging. A drill press was used to drill these buttons. Drill at a slow speed. Alternatively, you can use quick-setting epoxy resin and attach a bail finding to the top of the button. Sand the area to which the bail will be attached prior to applying the epoxy.

2. If desired you can clip off the button shank on the back if the particular button has one. This can be done with needle-nose pliers or wire cutters.

3. Cut images to fit the center of the button. Coat the cut images on all sides with decoupage glue using a flat brush; make sure to seal the edges of the paper, too. Waxed paper

is a good surface to work on and also provides a good place for the pieces to dry. Peel the images off the waxed paper after they dry.

4. Use more decoupage glue to attach the images to chip board. Cut around the images on the board after the glue dries. Seal the chip board with decoupage glue.

5. Press the coated image into the button. Make sure the decoupage glue is thoroughly dried. Mix the 2-part doming resin in a mixing cup with a stir stick (see directions on page 26–27). Use a stick to drop the resin over the image and fill the bezel to the top. Let the resin cure overnight. For a domed effect, mix a fresh batch of doming resin and layer it over the cured resin in the bezel. This resin has a surface tension that allows it to be applied to the edge without spilling over if you're careful not to coax it over the edge. Let the resin cure undisturbed overnight or until no longer tacky.

6. Embellish the chain with beads and other charms or decorations. In this example, beads were added to wire and then a wrapped loop was formed on each end with round-nose pliers to attach to the chain segments. Alternately you can make bead dangles with head pins and attach them to the chain with chain-nose pliers. To finish the necklace, use chain-nose pliers to attach a jump ring through the hole to hang the button from the chain. Add a clasp after you adjust the length of the necklace.

GREAT **HALLOWEEN** IMAGES
CAN BE FOUND ON **OLD VINTAGE**
POSTCARDS.

Froehliches Neu-Jahr.

Inspiration FALL INTO WINTER

Fall and winter are my favorite times of year. Fall is all about change, and I find that exciting. It triggers back-to-school memories from childhood: starting new classes, meeting up with friends, and of course shopping for new clothes and supplies for school.

The changes in nature inspire me the most: The way the shadows fall in the afternoon and the crisp, cool nights are some of my favorite sensory experiences. There are also smells that fill the air with the unmistakable scent of fall, such as the smell of cut fields during harvesttime and wood-burning stoves. Of course, other sure signs of fall are the amazing colors of the changing leaves and the fallen twigs and acorns. For me, all of this rich experience is inspiration for jewelry design.

Winter is also a very magical time of year. The ice, snow, and cool colors associated with winter provide an inspiring palette for jewelry making. Beads and stringing materials in cool blues, greens, and shades of white along with sparkly crystals work well together to create winter-themed pieces of jewelry.

Polymer Clay Acorn Charms

Through the ages the acorn has been a popular inspiration for jewelry designs. It has an appealing shape, and the cap has an interesting texture. Acorn themes are found in ancient architecture, ornaments, cutlery, and furniture. Although the acorn symbolizes many things historically in folklore, I like the acorn because it represents fall. The acorn is an appealing object to replicate by casting your own clay charms from a mold.

SUPPLIES

2-part silicone mold putty
Acorn
Paintbrush
Olive oil
Premo! Sculpey™ polymer clay in
    bronze, silver, gold, and white
    pearl (*Polyform Products Co.*)
X-ACTO® knife
Eye pins or wire loops

Pearl Ex Powered Pigments,
    metallic colors
Dust mask
Needle tool or toothpick
Plain paper
Glass baking dish
3 metal cords, each 12 inches in
    length (*Tinsel Trading Company*)
    or chain

Ruler
Cord crimp findings
2 chain-nose pliers
Clasp
Jump ring
Scissors

1. To make a mold of the acorn, pinch off and roll a small ball of each component of the mold putty. Mix the two parts thoroughly until the color of the putty is uniform (see directions on page 26). Quickly press the acorn into the putty, side down and halfway into the putty. Push the mold putty in around the acorn to make sure you get a good impression.

2. Make about three or four registration marks with the end of a paintbrush around the acorn. The registration marks will help you later to fit the two parts of the mold together, as the holes on one half will match the bumps of the other. Keep the acorn in place as the mold cures.

3. After the mold has cured (when you can press your fingernail into the mold and it will not leave a mark), use

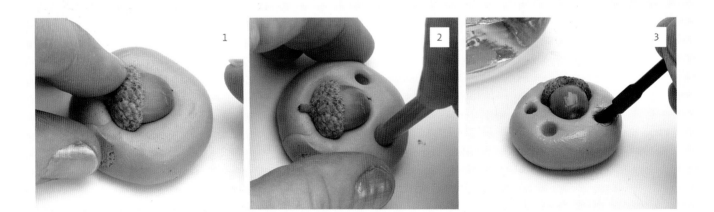

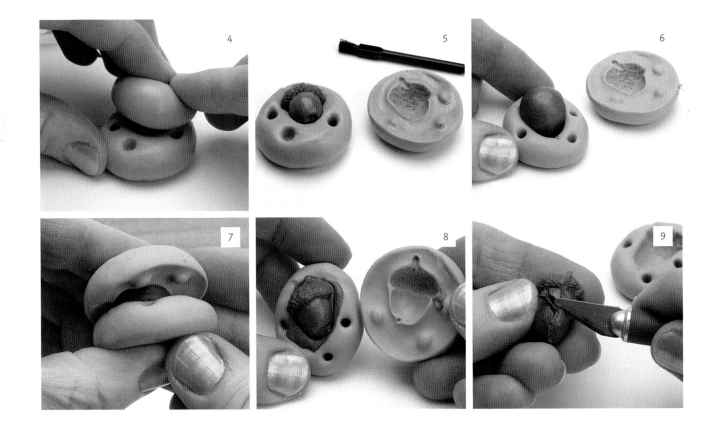

a paintbrush to apply olive oil to the exposed surface of the putty. Take care to brush the oil into the registration marks as well. This will act as a release agent for the second half of the mold. Don't move or disturb the acorn as you oil the mold.

4. Mix up more mold putty as you did in step 1 to form the top half of the mold. Press the mold putty over the bottom part of the acorn and the top half of the mold. Press well to make sure the mold putty surrounds the acorn and is pressed into the registration marks. Let the mold putty set until cured.

5. Remove the top half of the mold and remove the acorn.

6. To make the clay acorn charms, condition and mix colors of polymer clay to create a palette of muted

metallic colors. Metallic bronze clay was mixed with metallic silver, gold, and white pearl in various combinations to make coordinating hues in rich pearl and bronze tones. Roll a small ball of clay for the acorn, estimating the size. Place the ball of clay in the bottom half of the mold.

7. Press the top half of the mold over the clay and match the registration marks surrounding the acorn. Press the mold halves together well.

8. Open the mold and remove the clay acorn. You will see a clay seam around the clay acorn where the two molds met.

9. Trim off the seam with an X-Acto knife. Hint: It helps to cool the clay by placing it in the refrigerator to stiffen it a bit before trimming the seams. It's really hard to work

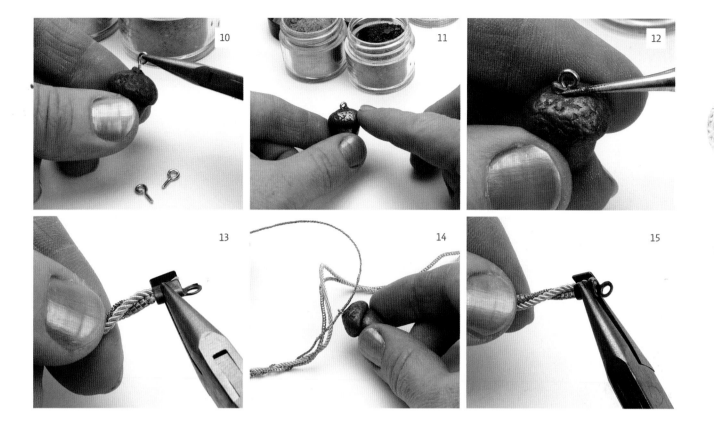

if the clay is too warm and therefore soft.

10. Embed an eye pin or wire loop into the clay. Bend the wire with your fingers or pliers in such a way that it won't pull out after baking.

11. For extra shimmer, use your finger to apply a little powdered pigment to the acorns. Wear a dust mask when working with these powders, as it's harmful to inhale the loose particles.

12. Use a needle tool or a toothpick to push the clay around the base of the loop to keep the loop securely in place. Bake the charms on a piece of plain paper on a glass baking dish for 30 minutes at 275 degrees Fahrenheit.

13. After baking and cooling the acorn charms, attach them to a cord or chain. To make a braided bracelet from metal cord, measure off about 12 inches for each of the three cords. Attach a cord crimp finding by using chain-nose pliers to crimp the finding over the ends of the three cords.

14. Braid the cords, slide the acorn charm onto one of the cords, and continue braiding until the cords are the correct length to fit around your wrist.

15. Clip off the ends of the cords with scissors and finish by crimping the other finding over the braided cord with chain-nose pliers. Add a clasp and jump ring for a closure.

Winter Solstice Charm Exchange Bracelet

I have friends who love making jewelry, too. We see one another at art retreats and other functions. One of the best parts of getting together is the show-and-tell and the sharing of new ideas and techniques. We also have a fun tradition of holding a charm exchange. One year the theme was an icy blue and white color palette. This bracelet features the charms from that exchange. The charm I made for it was created using primarily polymer clay and epoxy resin. The other charms were made by Adrienne Keith (beaded charms), Wendy Wallin Malinow (metal clay, glass, and mixed media), and Julie Collings (felted wool).

If you're interested in doing a charm swap, you might want to consider organizing your own or joining one of the numerous groups online that offer swaps. In case you don't know how an exchange or swap works, you make a specified number of pieces and then receive the same in return. One of the participants is usually the organizer, who then mails the finished charms and oversees the project. It's fun to look forward to receiving a parcel of handmade goodies in the mail on a cold winter day.

SUPPLIES

8 faceted crystal beads, 4 blue, 4 silver

7 head pins, silver

Base metal bezel finding with filigree edge

Round-nose pliers

Sobo® white glue (*PVA glue*)

Copied image

Mod Podge decoupage medium (*Plaid Creative Group*)

Flat brush

Waxed paper

Polymer clay, metallic silver

Glass baking dish

2-part epoxy resin

Graduated mixing cup

Stir stick

Toothpick

Glitter (*optional*)

Wire clippers

2 chain-nose pliers

Bracelet chain with clasp

Jump ring

1. To make the beaded deer charm, thread a silver bead onto a head pin. Then thread the head pin through one side of the bezel finding and out through the opposite side. Add another silver bead and then form a loop for hanging with round-nose pliers. Don't cut the end of the wire; it will be finished later.

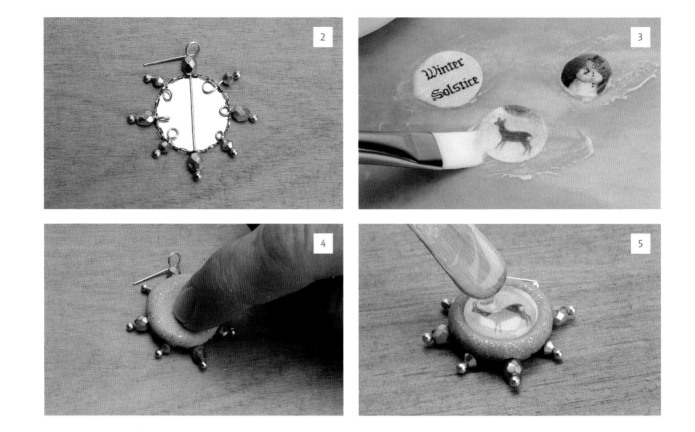

2. The next beads will be attached individually. Add a blue bead to a head pin and clip off the wire, leaving about ½ inch. Insert the wire through the filigree edge of the bezel and form a loop with round-nose pliers to secure the bead inside the bezel. Continue adding beads around the filigree edge, alternating bead colors. Coat the bottom of the bezel with white glue to secure the wire ends. Make sure the beads are pushed close to the outside edge of the bezel. Let the glue dry.

3. This project features a photocopied vintage image. Select the image of your choice, copy it, and then prepare the image by cutting it into a circle a little smaller than the inside of the bezel. Coat the back, front, and cut edge with decoupage glue using a flat brush. Waxed paper is helpful to work on. Let the glue dry.

4. Roll a small ball of clay to fit into the center of the bezel. Push the ball into the middle with your finger to make an indentation or a well for the image to sit in. Bake the piece at 275 degrees Fahrenheit for 30 minutes on a glass baking dish. Note: Be sure to follow manufacturer's safety warnings and avoid burning the clay.

5. Press the image into the center of the clay, gluing it in place with more decoupage glue if necessary. Let the glue dry thoroughly. Mix a small amount of 2-part epoxy resin in a mixing cup with a stir stick (see directions on pages 26–27). Use a toothpick to layer the epoxy resin over the image to fill the well. Sprinkle glitter into the wet resin to simulate snow if desired. Let the epoxy resin sit in a warm place until cured, at least 72 hours.

6. Refine the loop at the top of the finished charm for hanging using round-nose pliers.

7. Twist the end of the wire at the base of the loop and clip off the excess wire.

8. Use chain-nose pliers to pinch the end of the wire into the base of the wrapped work.

9. Using chain-nose pliers, attach the finished charm to the bracelet with a jump ring.

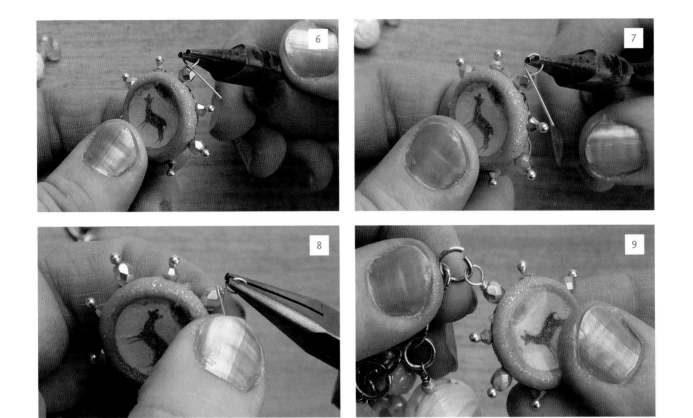

Collections

ig om oig sade ... an sleep saf... till m...ning, ...d their mother k...

Gå bort ur min åsyn,
ou är för mig en stöteste...
ou besinnar icke det Gud ...hö-
er, utan det menniskor ...uhörer.

Då sade Jesus till sina lär-
jungar: ... till efter-
ölja mig ... sig sjä...
och tage ... sig ...
ölje mi... en ...
vill ben... an sk...
...ista det, men ...vouten s...
...ister sitt lif för min ...u-
han skall finna det. Ty hw...
...kall det hjelpa en menni...
...m hon winner hela werld...
...en förlorar sin själ? E...
...wad k... menniska gif...
...ill löse...
Menni...
in ...
...ngla...
...ch ...
...San...
...åg ...
...a, ...
...Ren...

wardt forbanvlad m...
och hans ... sken såsom
solen, och hans kläder worv...
hwita såsom lj...t. Och s...
dem syntes Moses och Elias,
... the wood all night,

No. 826   Ithaca, N.Y.   Ap... 16

The Tompkins County N... Ban...

ESTABLISHED 1836.

Pay to
or   ...arket $5 ...

FOR RENT

...atch over good children.

Inspiration
FAIRY TALES AND FLOWERS

I enjoy collecting ephemera, greeting cards, and old children's books. Many of my favorite illustrators, including Arthur Rackham, Harrison Cady, Beatrix Potter, Jesse Willcox Smith, Sir John Tenniel, and Edwin Austin Abbey, were published during the "Golden Age" of illustration (from the 1880s until the end of World War I). These illustrators were classically trained, yet each had a distinct style. Their work still has a strong influence on illustrators today. Long before animation, a single illustration filled with remarkable detail would make a story come to life.

Early botanical watercolor paintings are another type of illustration that influences my work. Botanical illustrations are one of the earliest watercolor genres. They combine pen and ink with watercolor to depict plants and flowers in great detail, as if they were being viewed under a microscope. Botanical illustrations were often used in scientific textbooks to help herbalists and physicians; but in addition to being practical, these illustrations were often beautiful compositions that are truly pieces of art in their own right.

There are several well-known botanical illustrators whose works are still popular today. Albrecht Dürer is one of my favorite artists, and he painted some of the earliest examples of this style of illustration. Pierre-Joseph Redouté was a French painter who was the official court artist of Marie Antoinette and is considered the most famous botanical illustrator of his time. Another favorite of mine is Joris Hoefnagel, who is known for illuminated manuscripts and his multivolume book of natural history miniatures.

These illustrations lend themselves to inspire jewelry designs because of the meticulous attention paid to detail. There are many images in the public domain that can be used for a finished piece of jewelry. Use a small painting "as is" for a bezel, or you can study a painting to inspire a new design based on a favorite flower or plant. I transfer Redouté's rose paintings onto silver, and they always read well on the jewelry due to the clarity with which they were originally painted.

Resin Clay Flower Bracelets

I was inspired by a botanical illustration by Pierre-Joseph Redouté to create these clay flowers. The flowers are loosely fashioned after the roses depicted in his painting of Austrian Copper roses. The petals are open, more like a wild rose's than a formal hybrid tea rose's. The braided fabric wristband adds to the informal country charm of this climbing rose variety.

SUPPLIES

2-part epoxy resin clay
Sculpting tools
Acrylic paint
Small round paintbrush

Cloth or paper towel
Cotton fabric, 18 inches long
   by 6 inches wide
Scissors

Sewing needle
Thread
Button
Fabri-Tac Permanent Adhesive

1. Pinch off an equal-sized ball of epoxy resin clay and catalyst. You can mix your own custom colors prior to adding the catalyst, kneading the color together first before adding an equal amount of the catalyst portion. Mix the two components thoroughly until uniform in color (see directions on page 24).

2. Pinch off small balls of the clay and flatten them to make flower petals. Use your finger to form each petal into a cup shape. Make five large petals for the base of the flower and five small petals for the center of it.

3. Arrange the five large petals in a circle to make the flower and then add the five small petals to the center. It's helpful to wait for the clay to start to cure a bit, as the petals will hold their shape better. You can let the petals sit for about 20 minutes and then shape them.

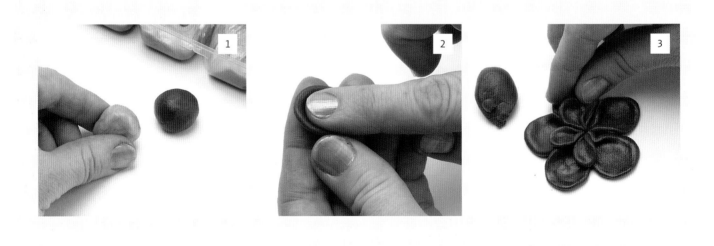

4. Mix another color of epoxy resin clay (for the center of the flower). Press the ball of clay into the center of the petals and use a pointed sculpting tool to make a texture. Use the tool to pierce two holes in the center if you wish to attach the finished piece by sewing it on to the bracelet like a button. If not, you can glue it in place with fabric glue. Let the clay cure overnight.

5. After the clay has cured, add details to the flower with acrylic paint. A darker color was added to the center of

this flower to add contrast.

6. Wipe off the paint with a cloth or paper towel to leave a "stain" in the recessed areas.

7. Paint finer details with a small round paintbrush.

8. Make the fabric bracelet by tearing the fabric into three strips, each 2 inches wide by 18 inches long. Make a snip with the scissors to get started, and then tear the strips the entire length of the fabric, tearing with the grain. Secure

the ends of all three strips with a knot and braid the strips together.

9. Leave the braid loose near the knot for the button to fit through.

10. Measure your wrist as you braid to determine the finished length. Sew through all thicknesses of the braided fabric to secure the ends. Sew a button onto the end of the finished braid. Cut off the excess fabric close to the button. Check the button for fit through the braided work on the opposite end.

11. Attach the flower to the center of the fabric bracelet with fabric glue. Let the glue dry overnight. Or if you chose to make holes in the flower in step 4, you can sew the flower in place as though it were a button.

12. To wear the bracelet, fasten the button through the braid as shown.

Fairy-Tale Bubble Necklace

My dad grew up with a love of books, and he believed in reading to my sister and I. He read to us frequently from a collection of favorite fairy tales and adventure stories he had saved from his own childhood. The best part about his stories was that my dad was a radio announcer, and used his radio voice to read the stories to us, complete with dramatic flair and different voices for each character. His voice was so much fun to listen to that it almost didn't matter what story he was reading. "Snow White and Rose Red" was one of my favorite stories as a child, I suppose not so much for the plot as for the charming illustrations and the colored jewels in the story. This necklace features illustrations from the book I owned as a child.

SUPPLIES

Vintage illustrations
Scissors
Acrylic cabochon, 1½-inch size
    (*Tapp Plastics, Inc.*)
Mod Podge decoupage medium
    (*Plaid Creative Group*)
Flat brush

Acrylic cabochon, ¾-inch or
    1-inch size (*optional*)
    (*Tapp Plastics, Inc.*)
Apoxie Sculpt 2-part epoxy resin
    clay (*Aves Studio*)
Leather stamping tool (*Tandy
    Leather Factory*) (*optional*)

Plastic-coated wire
Wire clippers
Round-nose pliers
Pointed-back rhinestones
Colored chain (*My ELEMENTS*)
Beads, glass or plastic
2 chain-nose pliers
Clasp

1. Copy the vintage illustrations to fit behind the cabochons. Cut the image to fit. Brush a layer of decoupage medium on the back of the cabochons in a thin layer using a flat brush.

2. Quickly press the image (facedown) over the larger cabochon, making sure to press out any bubbles. Wipe off the excess glue around the edges of the paper. Make a smaller cabochon in the same fashion to use as an accent bead if desired.

3. To surround the cabochon bubbles with clay, mix equal parts of the epoxy resin clay and catalyst. Mix the clay well (see directions on page 24). Divide the clay to use for each bubble. Roll the clay into a ball and make an impression with your finger in the clay for the bubble.

4. Place the bubble into the center of the clay.

5. Press the clay up around the base of the bubble to hold the bubble in place after the clay cures.

6. Use a leather stamping tool to make designs on the clay if desired.

7. Clip small pieces of plastic-coated wire to make loops. Form a loop with a twist at the base, which will keep the wire securely embedded in the clay. Push the twisted loops into the clay. These will be used for hanging the necklace or for attaching the accent beads. Place the wires accordingly.

7

8. To add sparkle, push pointed-back rhinestones into the clay. Push them deeply into the clay to hold.

9. You can make accent beads out of the epoxy resin clay to embellish the necklace. Form clay shapes over wire pieces, texturing them or embedding rhinestones. Suspend them over a lid or other object as they cure. Let all the pieces cure overnight. To finish the necklace, use the wire and the chain to connect the pieces, adding beads to the wire. Use round-nose pliers to make wrapped-wire loops and connect them to the chain and wire with chain-nose pliers. Add a clasp to the chain with chain-nose pliers.

Inspiration BEADS, BUTTONS, AND CHARMS

Many people who like to make jewelry share a passion for collecting small things. With the popularity of assembling found objects to make jewelry, even broken pieces can be salvaged to create fabulous new designs. I collect antique buttons, glass beads, Lucite charms, and old plastic miniatures, including Cracker Jack charms.

My fascination with plastic miniatures began with the German-made figurines my mother would buy from our local dime store, Sprouse Reitz. The store itself brings back fond memories; they had all sorts of unusual craft items along with everything else you can imagine, and they always had popcorn at the front counter. My mom crafted egg ornaments, and she used the tiny miniatures she purchased there to create intricate scenes inside the eggs. These hand-painted hard-plastic figurines from Germany are exquisite, and some of them continue to be made today using the same molds and manufacturing techniques that were used more than seventy years ago.

Cracker Jack charms are as endearing as the German figurines. They predate my childhood, but you can find antique toy charms on sites such as eBay or in antique shops. The early charms are made of celluloid, cardboard, or metal. Other plastics and materials were used later. Gum ball machine toys are also collectible and make cute charms for retro-style jewelry pieces.

More than a few people I know fell into an instant collection of vintage beads or buttons either given to them or inherited from a grandmother or aunt. Glass jars or tins filled with buttons and beads hold a special meaning if they carry a personal history. Even if you're not lucky enough to have some handed down to you, you can purchase old beads and buttons from online auctions or antique dealers, and at flea markets or yard sales.

Antique Button Pendants

These pendants are made using antique metal buttons featuring embossed designs such as flowers, fruits, or animals, just to name a few. I have a background in sewing and have always been attracted to buttons. The fact that buttons are functional as well as decorative makes them perfect for jewelry. Choose beads, chains, and findings to coordinate with the button of choice to be used for the focal point of the necklace.

SUPPLIES

Vintage button, brass or metal
Heavy-duty wire cutters
Awl or piercing tool
Metal hole punch

Chain
Jump ring
2 chain-nose pliers
Beads

Round-nose pliers
Wire clippers
Head pins
Clasp

1. Remove the shank from the back of the button with heavy-duty wire cutters.

2. Mark the placement of the holes at the top of the button as well as the bottom (if you want to hang a bead dangle from the button) with an awl or other piercing tool. Then use a metal hole punch to make holes. There are different types of punches for metal. This one tightens down into the metal by turning a screw punch through a die that then punches through the metal.

3. Another type of punch forces the metal through a die as you squeeze the handle. It punches through metal as thick as a coin. Choose a die to correspond to the size of the finished hole you want to make.

4. To attach the button to a chain, open a jump ring with chain-nose pliers and attach the button to the chain.

5. Close the jump ring (see directions on page 23).

6. Add beads to embellish the chain, using head pins to attach the beads to the chain. Form a loop at the end of each head pin with round-nose pliers. Attach the loop to the chain and twist the wire around the base of the loop to secure. Clip off the excess wire with wire clippers.

7. Optional: To add a bead dangle to the bottom of the button, add beads to a head pin and form a loop at the top of the head pin to attach it through the hole at the base of the button. Using round-nose pliers, twist the end of the head pin around the base of the formed loop after attaching the wire to the button. Clip off the excess wire. Add a clasp with chain-nose pliers to finish after cutting the wire to the desired length.

Lucite Flower Bracelets

My love of color and floral design inspired these designs. The Lucite flower beads used in this project have sharp details and vibrant colors that make these collectible pieces appealing. Lucite is a plastic that was developed by Dupont in 1937. It can be clear, tinted with color, or opaque. Collected flower shapes and beads were combined to create these colorful retro-style bracelets. You can find Lucite charms and flowers at antique fairs and from online auction sites, as well as in some bead shops.

Lucite Flower Bracelets

SUPPLIES

Lucite plastic flowers with holes in
    the center of each

Charm bracelet chain with clasp

Round beads, glass or plastic

Head pins

Round-nose pliers

Wire clippers

Chain-nose pliers

1. Arrange clusters of coordinating color combinations for the flowers. Make stacked designs with larger pieces on the bottom and either one or two smaller flowers placed on top. Arrange them along a charm bracelet chain to create a pleasing composition.

2. Slide a bead onto a head pin for the center of the flower or use a decorative head pin for the center. After the bead is added, thread the flower pieces onto the head pin.

3. Form a loop on the back with the wire using round-nose pliers. This loop will be used to attach the flower cluster to the chain. Leave the loop open for now.

4. Repeat steps 2 and 3 to make a series of flower clusters on head pins for the chain. Attach each cluster by attaching the formed loop to the chain.

5. Finish each loop by twisting the end of the wire of the head pin around the base of the loop.

6. Clip off the excess wire and tuck the end of the wire in with the tip of the chain-nose pliers. Add extra beads if desired along the chain to add bulk to the bracelet. Use the round-nose and chain-nose pliers to attach the beads in the same manner as you attached the flowers.

Vintage Glass Bead Earrings

When you're collecting beads, it's hard to tell which are vintage and which are new. Serious collectors often buy beads directly from the source: dealers or factories in the Czech Republic or in other places, such as Austria or Germany. You can also find vintage glass beads that were made in Japan. Many glass beads are still made using the same molds and glassmaking techniques that were used in years past. This makes them readily available and affordable.

Using beads with certain findings, especially antique pieces, will give them a vintage look whether they are new or old. Keep in mind that actual vintage beads will cost more than new beads, so make sure you know what you are paying for if possible. I collect beads by choosing colors I like rather than worrying about whether they are actually old stock. Sometimes you find a certain color you can't find anywhere else, and it inspires a great design. The following three earrings designs (pictured below) each feature a distinct wire- wrapping technique. Once you learn a few basics, you can make simple earrings with any type of bead.

Cascading Violet Crystal and Pearl Earrings

SUPPLIES

2 faceted crystal beads, 6–8mm

8 brass head pins

2 filigree bead caps

Round-nose pliers

Chain

Wire cutters

6 small pearls

2 brass ear wire loops

2 chain-nose pliers

1. Slide a faceted crystal bead onto a head pin, followed by a filigree bead cap.

2. Form a loop at the top of the bead cap with round-nose pliers; don't finish wrapping the loop until it has been attached to the chain in step 3.

3. Cut a small length of chain (five or six links) with wire cutters and attach the loop to the chain.

4. Hold the loop with chain-nose pliers and wrap the head pin around the base of the loop after attaching it to the chain. Clip off the excess wire.

5. Slide a pearl onto each head pin, form a loop with round-nose pliers, and attach the loop to the chain with chain-nose pliers in the same fashion as the crystal was attached in steps 2 and 4.

6. After attaching three pearls or additional beads if desired, add an ear wire loop to the end of the chain as shown to finish the earring. Use chain-nose pliers to open and close the loop of the ear wire. Ear wire loops should be opened and closed in the same way as jump rings (see directions on page 23).

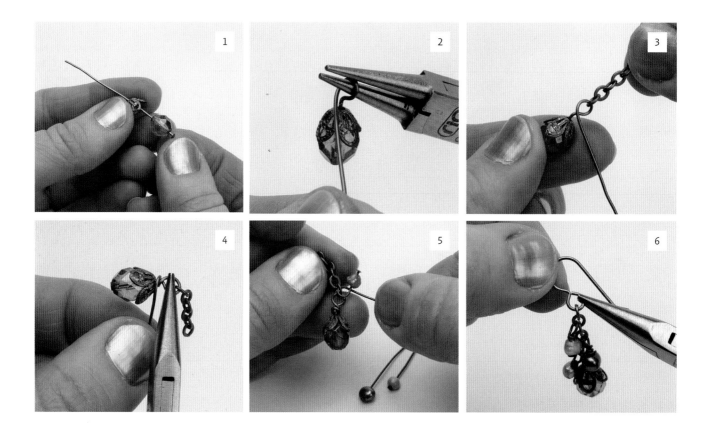

Briolette Stone Earrings with Bead Accents

SUPPLIES

2 pieces of 24-gauge dead soft
    sterling silver wire, each
    12 inches in length
    (*Thunderbird Supply Company*)

2 faceted briolette stone beads
    (*side drilled at the pointed end*)
Round-nose pliers
2 chain-nose pliers

Wire cutters
2 stone beads
2 ear wire loops

1. Thread the silver wire through the briolette, leaving about 1½ inches remaining on one side. Bend the sides of the wire toward the center top with round-nose pliers, crossing one side over the other.

2. Hold the wires with chain-nose pliers as shown. This will give you more control as you wrap the wire. Wrap the shorter side around the longer one with a few wraps using round-nose pliers. Keep the longer side straight from the center top of the briolette.

3. After wrapping, clip off the excess wire from the shorter end.

4. Thread a stone bead onto the wire.

5. Using round-nose pliers, form a loop with the wire, wrapping the wire around the stem until you reach the bead.

6. Clip off the excess wire with wire cutters.

7. Use chain-nose pliers to pinch the end of the wire at the base of the wrapped wire and to tuck in the end and hide it.

8. Attach an ear wire loop to finish the earring. Use chain-nose pliers to close the loop on the earring. Repeat the above steps for the second earring.

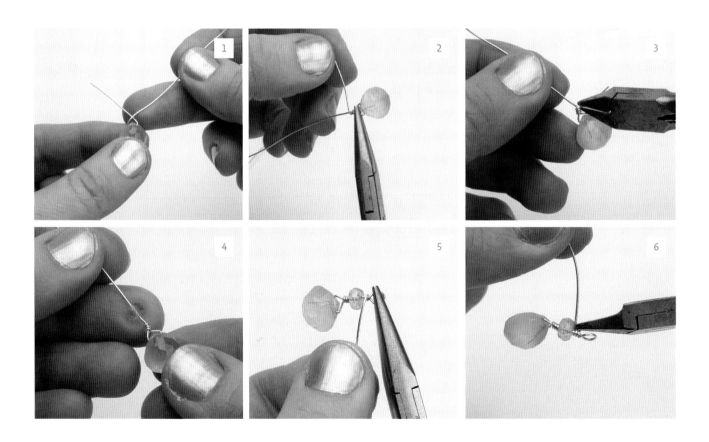

7

8

Wrapped-Wire Briolette Bead Earrings

SUPPLIES

2 pieces of 24-gauge dead soft
   sterling silver wire, each
   12 inches in length
   (*Thunderbird Supply Company*)

2 faceted briolette stone beads
   (*side drilled at the pointed end*)
Round-nose pliers
2 chain-nose pliers

Wire cutters
2 ear wire loops

1. Thread the silver wire through the briolette, leaving about 1½ inches remaining on one side. Bend the sides of the wire toward the center top with round-nose pliers, crossing one side over the other.

2. Hold the wire with chain-nose pliers as shown. This will give you more control as you wrap the wire. Wrap the shorter side around the longer one with a few wraps using round-nose pliers. Keep the longer side straight from the center top of the briolette.

3. After wrapping, clip off the excess wire from the shorter end.

4. Using round-nose pliers, form a loop with the wire near the top of the wrapped section.

5. Wrap the wire back down to the top of the bead, covering the wrapped section of the shorter side. You can continue wrapping over the top of the bead if desired.

6. Clip off the excess wire with wire cutter, and use chain-nose pliers to pinch the end of the wire at the base of the wrapped wire to tuck in the end and hide it. Attach an ear wire loop to finish the earring. Use chain-nose pliers to close the loop on the earring. Repeat the above steps for the second earring.

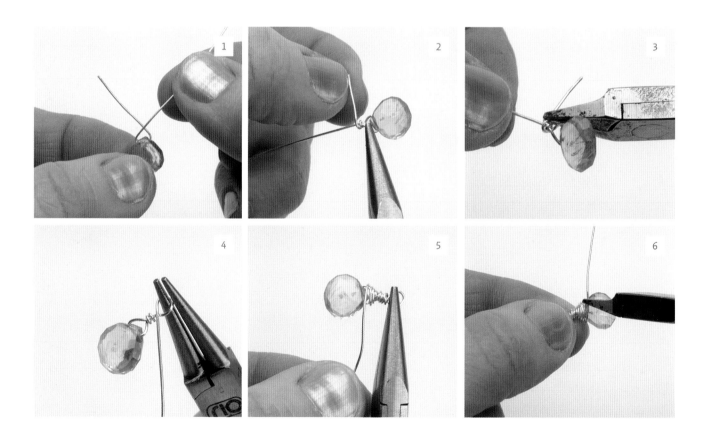

Cracker Jack Charm Bracelet

I've always had a fascination with tiny objects. I remember how much fun it was as a child to find small treasures in Cracker Jack boxes. The prizes were cool, three-dimensional toys and I wish I had saved some of them. The toys were replaced with paper prizes in more recent times. Cracker Jack toys were introduced in 1893, and by 1912 toy prizes were included in boxes.

The small toys are now highly collectible and you can find them on sites such as eBay. Add jump rings to old toy charms to make a bracelet, or replicate the charms by casting them from hand-made molds. You can cast new charms using silver-, bronze-, or copper-type clays to make metal versions of old plastic favorites.

SUPPLIES

Found or collected charms, vintage Cracker Jack or gum ball machine charms

Sterling silver bracelet chain and

clasp or purchased sterling silver bracelet chain with clasp attached

2 chain-nose pliers

Liver of Sulfur or Black Max (*optional*)

Pro-Polish Polishing Pads (*Rio Grande®*)

Jump rings

SUPPLIES FOR MAKING YOUR OWN CLAY CHARM REPRODUCTIONS

3-D charm

2-part silicone mold putty

Tool to make registration marks (*e.g., end of paintbrush*)

Olive oil

PMC3 silver clay

Sandpaper or a nail file

Hook (*fine silver wire or brass if firing with metal clay*)

Liver of Sulfur or Black Max

Pro-Polish Polishing Pads (*Rio Grande*)

1. Choose charms that coordinate well together to arrange on the bracelet chain. Vintage Cracker Jack toys make excellent charms, as they are incredibly detailed and have a hole at the top for hanging.

2. To prepare the silver chain before assembling it, add a clasp to it to fit your wrist using chain-nose pliers, or use a purchased bracelet. If your chain is new and shiny, you may want to patina the chain to darken it. Use Liver of Sulfur (see directions on page 29). This will give your chain a nice antique look that is perfectly suited to the charms.

3. Use a jump ring to connect the charm to the chain. Use chain-nose pliers to open the jump ring and then attach it to the chain (see page 23).

4. Close the jump ring with chain-nose pliers. Continue to add other charms until the chain is as full as you wish.

5. To make your own replicas of vintage charms, you can mold them easily. Start with a full, round, dimensional charm such as the black plastic Scottie dog shown here. Follow the directions on page 26 for making a 2-part silicone mold. This photo shows the finished mold. Silver metal clay was placed in the mold to cast the final piece. Prior to firing the piece the seam was refined and sanded off with a small nail file or sandpaper, and a silver wire hook was embedded in the top for hanging.

5

6

6. Fire the piece as directed for metal clay. After the charm is burnished to make it nice and shiny, a patina solution of Liver of Sulfur or Black Max (see directions page 29) was applied to it. The highlights are buffed away with a silver-polishing pad. The patina will remain in the recessed areas, which will bring out the details. Make a series of charms to add to a charm bracelet or attach a single charm to a chain using a jump ring to make a necklace.

Blast
from
the
Past

Inspiration JUST ONE WORD: PLASTICS

There was a wave of plastic crafts that were popular in the early '70s. Polyester resin was used to make household items such as paperweights, penholders, key chains, and grapes for the coffee table. Aside from the grapes, I remember my dad pouring resin into large molds to make animal shapes to hang on my wall. I also recall him rushing to open all of the windows to air out the house to get rid of the awful chemical fumes. Different types of resin are now sold that allow you to make similar projects but with fewer chemical fumes. New formulations are easier to mix, measure, and use than older polyester types, allowing you to make colorful retro-style baubles.

Another plastic craft that was popular in the '70s was shrink plastic. I remember making shrink art jewelry before the product was sold commercially. We would buy "liver lids" from the meat department at the grocery store. The lids were clear plastic with red stripes around the edge. Liver used to come in the plastic container that the lid fit. When heated in the oven, the lids shrank to pendant-sized pieces with nifty red-striped borders. We traced comic book characters with Sharpie® permanent markers and cut them out, punched holes in them, and then watched them curl up in the oven as they shrank into little charms. The finished pieces were attached to charm bracelets with jump rings.

The first commercially available shrink plastic product was sold under the brand name Shrinky Dinks®. It was manufactured in sheet form and was launched in the early '70s. It's now available in pre-sanded sheets, which gives you more options for adding color to the plastic. It's also available in a few colors and in a version that is made for ink jet printers, allowing you to print images and photos onto the plastic.

Although jewelry trends and styles change over time, plastic is always represented in some form. New designers have emerged who use old techniques with a fresh twist, which as a jewelry craftsperson is inspiring to see.

Rock 'n' Roll Shrink Art Necklaces

My favorite music genre is rock; I grew up listening to Boston, Journey, Rush, Foreigner, Heart, and Fleetwood Mac. Stevie Nicks from Fleetwood Mac is a favorite of mine, and I like the themes and lyrics in her songs. Her wardrobe style is legendary. She created her own visual style by wearing long, flowing dresses, shawls, capes in crimson and black, lots of lace, ribbons, and her signature suede platform boots. For these necklaces, I chose bold red and black with roses, birds, and heart designs to represent the edgy yet feminine side of rock 'n' roll that I so love. The retro–rock 'n' roll style has become increasingly popular in recent times and can be found on T-shirts tattoo art, and in jewelry design. The rose design is by Marina Collings.

SUPPLIES

Shrinky Dinks Ruff N'Ready pre-sanded shrink art plastic
Printed designs
Acrylic paint or colored pencils
Water
Paintbrush
Sharpie black permanent marker— fine tip

Scissors
⅛-inch round-hole punch (*optional*)
Plain paper
Baking sheet or glass baking dish
Beads
Head pins
Round-nose pliers

Wire cutters
Jump rings
Chain-nose pliers
Necklace chain with clasp

1. Start with your Shrinky Dinks plastic. If you choose to add color to the art, you can paint the rough surface of the plastic prior to tracing the design with a permanent marker. Or you can trace the image first and fill in with paint, like a coloring book. Water down the acrylic paint so it has a thin consistency and is very transparent; it will intensify and darken after the plastic shrinks. Alternately, you can use colored pencils, such as Prismacolor® brand, which work very well.

2. Copy the images to trace, keeping in mind that they will shrink to ⅓ of the original size. Trace a line drawing with the permanent marker. Use a fine tip for fine details. Trace the outline on either side of the plastic; in this example, the tracing was done on the rough side of the plastic.

3. Cut around the shape with scissors. For tight corners, make several small clips rather than turning the scissors in one motion, as this tears the plastic.

4. Punch holes in the plastic with a small round-hole punch.

5. Place the pieces on a piece of paper on a baking sheet or a glass baking dish. Bake the pieces at 300 degrees Fahrenheit for about 5 minutes or until they shrink and flatten completely. You can watch the process with the oven light on.

6. After the pieces are cool, add beads with head pins to the plastic. Use round-nose pliers to make the loops and to twist the wire to secure them. Clip off the excess wire. Attach the pieces to the chain using wrapped-wire loops (see page 23) or jump rings. Add a clasp if needed.

Resin Heart Pendants

This chunky heart pendant was made using a low-odor resin that mixes in equal parts, which makes it easier to use than the casting resins of the past. The resin can be left clear, or dyes and pigments can be added for color. Mix in glitter and sequins to create variations of the finished cast heart. The design was inspired by the desire to replicate the look of earlier Bakelite and Lucite plastic pieces, which are highly collectible. My fascination with how things are made is what often drives me to create a new design.

Resin Heart Pendants

SUPPLIES

Heart-shaped found object or
    handmade model made with
    polymer clay or epoxy resin clay
2-part silicone mold putty
2-part casting epoxy resin or
    polyurethane resin
Graduated mixing cups

Stir sticks
Red powdered pigment or liquid
    dye specifically for resin
Glitter
Dust mask
100–200 grit sandpaper or large
    emery board

320, 400, 600, 800, 1000, and 1200
    grit wet/dry sandpaper
Shallow pan
Craft hand drill (*FISKARS*)
Drill bit, 2mm or larger
Old phone book or catalog
Leather cord

1. Start with a found heart-shaped object, or you can make your own using polymer clay or epoxy resin clay. If you use polymer clay, follow the manufacturer's instructions to sculpt and bake the clay heart. Note: Be sure to follow manufacturer's safety warnings and avoid burning the clay. If you use epoxy resin clay, it will cure without baking. Estimate how much mold putty you will need, and roll an equal-sized ball of each component of the silicone mold putty. Mix the two parts together until you have a uniform color and the putty is mixed (see directions on page 26). Quickly press the heart into the putty and push the putty around the sides of heart to make the mold. Let the putty sit until cured.

2. Remove the heart model from the mold. The mold putty should continue to cure for a few days before you pour in the epoxy resin. Otherwise, you will have lots of bubbles in the resin, as the mold continues to outgas for some time.

3. To mix the epoxy resin, use a mixing cup and carefully pour in equal amounts of resin and catalyst. Mix thoroughly for about 1 minute (see directions on page 26-27). Mix a second cup of resin. Add a few drops of powdered pigment or liquid dye to the mixed resin. Mix the colorant with the resin well. You should have a cup of clear resin and another cup of tinted red resin.

4. Pour the clear resin into the mold.

5. Use a stir stick to swirl some of the red resin into the clear.

6. Add glitter or other inclusions before the resin cures. Let the resin cure in a warm place until it can be tapped with a stick and is no longer soft. This will take between 24 and 72 hours. Remove the heart from the mold.

7. Wear a dust mask when sanding. Start sanding the edges of the resin with a coarse (100–200 grit) sandpaper, and use the first grit dry to remove most of the unwanted rough edges. A large emery board will also work well. Now switch to wet sanding. Sand underwater in a shallow pan. This method will collect the dust and keep the resin from embedding back into the surface as you sand. Start your underwater sanding with 320 grit sandpaper, working progressively through each grit until most of the scratches are removed (1200 grit is the finest). You can get higher grits at auto body supply stores if you want to move even finer for a smoother finish.

8. To make a hole through the top of the heart, use a hand drill with a large enough bit to make a hole that the cord will fit through. Drill slowly through the cured resin to keep the plastic from melting on the bit. Have a helper hold the piece firmly on an old phone book or catalog as you drill.

9. Loop a cord through the hole to hang the heart. To make an adjustable closure, tie a knot over the right side with the left cord and then tie a knot over the left side with the right cord. If tied correctly, the knots should fit snugly together when pulled next to each other.

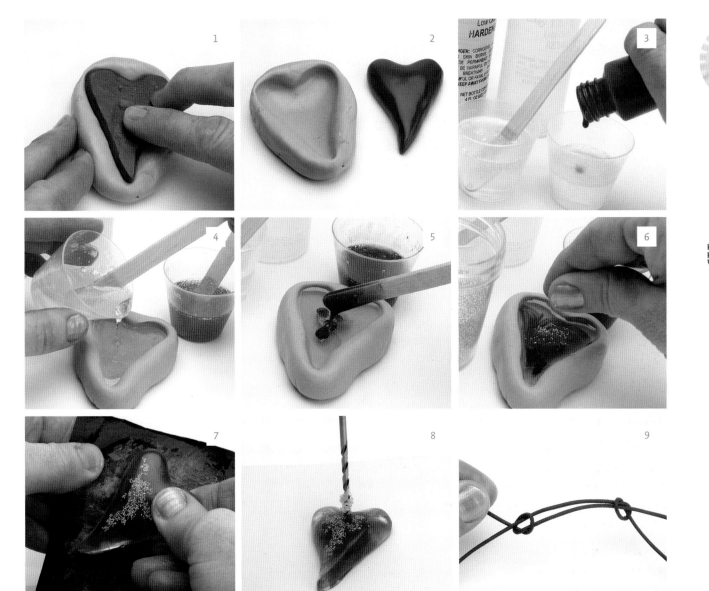

Inspiration GETTING GROOVY WITH FIBER

Textile and fiber arts include weaving, sewing, knitting, crochet, and macramé. All of these traditional fiber arts can be incorporated into jewelry designs. I like to use soft materials such as felt or fabric combined with chain and metal to make mixed-media designs. You can combine fiber techniques within the same piece—for example, using macramé knots to connect fabric pieces for a necklace design.

Most people think of jute plant hangers when you mention macramé. I made my share of them in the early '70s. Macramé and weaving were big back then, with plenty of examples that come to mind, such as owl or tree wall hangings, macramé vests, and hemp bracelets and chokers. With the variety of fibers available today, you can tie the same knots used for weaving and macramé to make contemporary pieces using materials such as silk, novelty fibers, and waxed linen, to name just a few. Rather than use typical wood or ceramic beads for macramé, you can choose from among a variety of large-holed beads available in silver, copper, or brass. There are also updated versions of wood and ceramic types with a more sophisticated look than the beads you used at camp. With the invention of metal clay, you can now make your own beads with holes large enough to fit over any size cord or fiber. Polymer and epoxy resin clay are also good choices for making colorful beads to coordinate with the fibers you use in a design.

Stick-Woven Fiber Bracelet

I love working with yarn and fibers, whether it be knitting, crochet, or weaving. In this project I incorporate fiber and textile arts with jewelry making. This is a very casual design made with earth-toned fiber colors and finished with a large, wood-style button. The fibers are woven over tapered sticks that have a hole at the end of each stick. You could make your own weaving sticks by drilling a hole at the base of wooden dowels. In a pinch you can also use plastic straws to weave fibers around. For variations on this design, use textured fibers embellished with cabochons or beads sewn or glued onto the finished cuff.

SUPPLIES

Beadsmith® hemp cord (*20 lb./9m*), 10 yards (*1 spool*)	Large-eyed blunt needle
4 weaving sticks	Scissors
1 ball or skein yarn or cord of your choice	Large button
	White fabric glue or fabric sealant

1. Double the warp cord and thread the two strands through the weaving sticks. Leave 1 yard long at each end and 1 yard in length between each stick. Gather the sticks and hold them in a row.

2. Knot the weaving (weft) yarn to one of the outside sticks. Weave the yarn over one stick and under the next, working an over-and-under pattern along the row of sticks. Work the yarn tail into the work as you weave.

3. When you reach the end of the row, bring the yarn around the last stick.

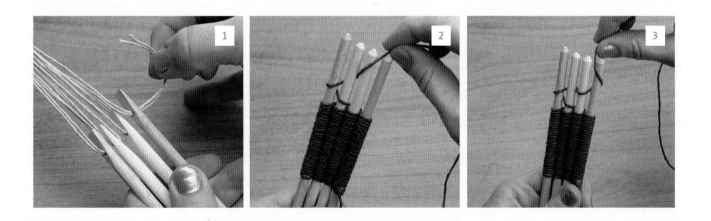

4. Continue weaving over and under the sticks. Follow this sequence, weaving to cover the sticks. Maintain a nice, even tension by keeping the sticks close together and pulling the yarn evenly.

5. As you cover the sticks, slide the sticks up out of the work, letting the woven yarn cover the warp cords threaded at the bottom. Continue weaving over the sticks and moving the work down over the warp cords. You will probably want to weave a longer length than you think you need, as the woven work will appear more spread out on the sticks. Once removed from the sticks it becomes much more compact in length. You can always unwind the extra yarn, but it's hard to weave in more length once the work is removed from the sticks.

6. When you have reached the desired length to fit around your wrist, slide the work onto the warp cord and off of the sticks.

7. Pull on the sticks to get rid of the slack in the loops at the base of the weaving. You should only see a double cord on each side that was left longer at the start.

8. Use a large-eyed needle to thread one of the long ends of cords through the weaving on the opposite side. This will form the loop that will pass over the button for the closure. After the cord is threaded along the length of the weaving, pull it to adjust the loop to fit over the button.

9. Cut the cord from the weaving sticks at the other end of the bracelet. Tie a square knot (see directions on page 30–31) with the cords from two of the sticks including the same cords that were just brought through to form the loop on the opposite end. Secure the knot, pulling tight. Repeat the same square knot with the cords from the other two sticks.

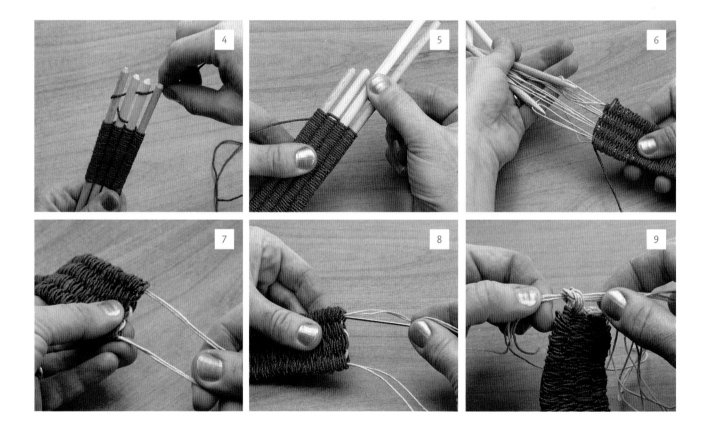

10. To make the knotted pattern over the loop for the button closure, use the long cord that is left at one end. Tie a series of lark's head knots over the loop cord (see directions on page 30–31). When the cord is covered with the knots, use the large-eyed needle to thread the cord tail back into the weaving and knot it on a cord hidden inside the weaving. Hide the cord tail inside the weaving and clip off the excess cord.

11. Tie a button to the remaining cords, knotting the cords on the back side of the weaving. Or you can sew the button on with thread if the cords aren't long enough.

12. Clip off the excess cord ends and secure the cords with white fabric glue or fabric sealant. Hide the cord tails inside the woven work.

Spool Knit Wire Bracelet

When I was a child I had a set of plastic spool knitters that I used to make clothes for dolls. I used yarn to form "knitted tubes," which were made into doll hats and tube-style shirts and dresses for Barbie®-sized dolls. A spool knitter is referred to as a "Knitting Nancy" or a "French Knitter." The homemade type consisted of a wooden spool with four nails hammered into the top, while the ones sold in stores were often colorfully painted figures or mushrooms. This project uses the same technique to make a sophisticated bracelet using sterling silver wire instead of yarn. Add pearls or beads to the design to embellish the bracelet even more.

SUPPLIES

28- or 26-gauge craft wire
Soft Flex® 5-pin knitting spool
    (*Soft Flex Company*)
Steel crochet hook, size 8 / 1.4mm
28-gauge fine silver wire, 3 feet
Safety pin (*optional*)
Wire cutters

Wire drawplate
    (*Soft Flex Company*)
18-gauge half-hard round sterling
    silver wire
Round-nose pliers
2 end caps with holes in top
Chain-nose pliers

S clasp or clasp of choice
Crystal slider beads or beads of
    your own choosing (*optional*)
Pearls (*optional*)
Chain-nose pliers

TIP: It's a good idea to start the work with a nonprecious metal wire. This allows you to practice a bit and to get a nice, even tension to begin with. After working on several rows, you can add fine silver to the spool. The how-to photos use a heavier, plastic-coated wire for demonstration purposes only; use a finer-gauge craft wire than is shown in the photos to start this project.

1. Start by using a 26- or 28-gauge craft wire before adding silver if you want to practice. Begin by wrapping the wire around the first peg of the knitting spool as shown. Leave a wire tail a few inches long tucked down inside the spool and wrap the working end of the wire around each individual peg in a clockwise direction (moving from peg to peg will follow a counterclockwise progression). If you are left-handed, work the wire in the opposite direction.

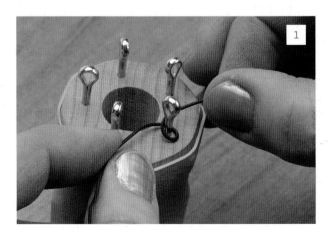

2. Continue to wrap each peg with one wrap (clockwise wrap), working around from peg to peg in a counterclockwise direction.

3. All five pegs will have one wrap as shown.

4. For the next round, bring the wire in front of the next peg; don't wrap it around the peg as you did to cast on.

5. With your other hand, hold the end of the wire against the spool directly opposite from the wire on the spool to keep it taut (this photo shows the left hand holding the wire against the spool on the opposite side). Use the crochet hook to bring the wire loop from below over the new wire.

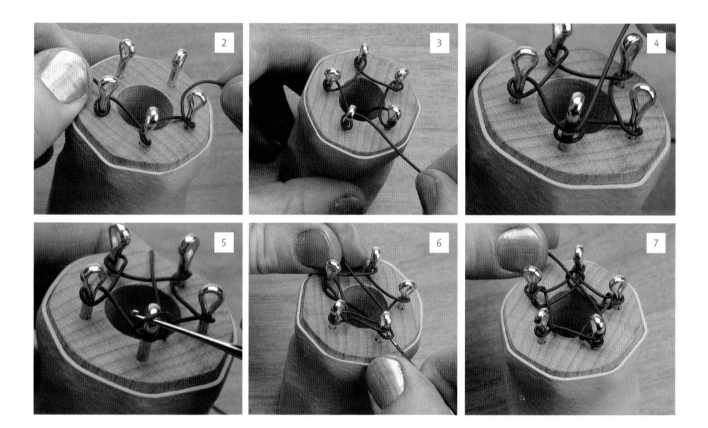

6. Continue bringing the wire around the front of each peg and hooking the bottom wire on the peg up and over the top wire and the peg, leaving only the new wire on the peg. The knitted pattern will start to form down the inside of the spool.

7. Continue around the spool, hooking each previous bottom loop over the new wire. Each is formed one at a time.

8. To add the 28-gauge silver wire, leave a tail of the practice wire inside the spool and start working the new wire around the pegs, as shown by the orange wire in the photo. (The orange wire is used simply for ease in illustrating the technique.)

9. With the crochet hook, lift a loop over the new wire; repeat around the pegs.

10. After all of the pegs are wrapped with the new wire, continue following the same pattern of lifting the previous loop over the new wire on each peg. This is the same method as shown in the previous steps. The practice wire section will be cut off later. Pull the work from the bottom from all sides with the crochet hook to pull it down inside the center of the tube.

11. This photo shows the silver wire in progress. If the wire is hard to pull over the peg, you can give it a firm tug to pull the bottom wire over the peg. If the new wire accidentally slips off of the peg, use the crochet hook to pull the wire back onto the peg.

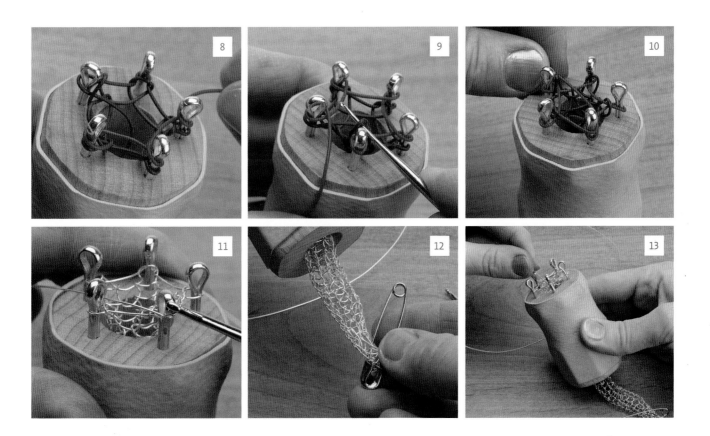

12. Keep working around the spool to form the tubular chain. You can attach a safety pin to the end of the work and use this to pull down the chain. Check the length as you progress.

13. Keep working until you have about 5 inches of work done. You will gain about ⅓ inch in length after the wire is pulled through the drawplate. The final length depends on the size of your wrist. You can always create a longer chain and then cut it into sections for several bracelet pieces.

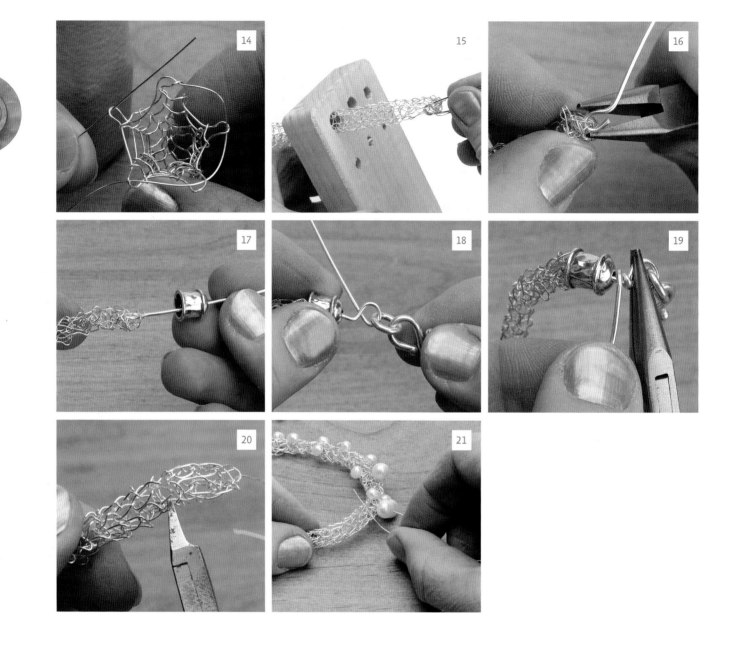

14. To cast off, clip the wire with wire cutters, leaving a few inches of wire on the end. Remove the wire from the pegs and run this wire through each loop to secure the round. Pull the wire to gather the loops.

15. To make the chain even, pull it through the drawplate, starting with the practice wire end. Pull the chain through the largest hole first. Progressively pull it through smaller holes until it's the right width to fit your end caps.

16. To add the end caps, make a loop at the end of the 18-gauge wire using round-nose pliers and hook it through the finished end of the chain. Close the loop with chain-nose pliers.

17. Thread an end cap onto the wire and pull it over the end of the knitted chain to cover. Pull snugly to make sure the chain is seated in the cap.

18. Bend the wire at a 90-degree angle with chain-nose pliers. Form a loop with round-nose pliers and attach the clasp.

19. Wrap the wire around the base of the loop to finish. Clip off the excess wire. You can add cylinder slider beads over the chain (see step 18 of the Viking Knit Wire Bracelet on page 126) at this point or alternately use 28-gauge wire to sew beads along the chain after the other end cap is attached, as explained in step 21.

20. Measure the bracelet to your wrist and then clip
off the end chain. Tuck the loose wires into the center,
removing any loose pieces of wire. Loop a piece of
18-gauge wire through the cut end and attach the other
end cap as you did in steps 16 and 17 to finish the bracelet.

21. You can add pearls by using the 28-gauge wire to sew
the beads into the chain. Anchor the wire into the work
using chain-nose pliers. Add a pearl and then bring the
wire back into the work, pulling the wire through to
secure the pearl. Continue adding pearls to cover the
chain as desired.

Viking Knit Wire Bracelet

This is another method of knitting wire that is similar to spool knitting. Instead of working around pegs to form a tubular chain, you form a chain around the outside of a wooden dowel. Loops are formed around the dowel and then the wire is threaded through each to form a pattern. The tube is then pulled through a drawplate to refine and lengthen the chain. This project was inspired by Northwest artist Tracy Stanley, who makes beautifully beaded versions of this Viking knit wire technique. She sells jewelry-making kits from her website: www.wiredarts.net.

SUPPLIES

24-gauge copper or dead soft
    sterling silver wire, 7 yards
    (*Thunderbird Supply Company*)
Credit card
Wooden dowel ³⁄₈ inch diameter
    by 6 inches long
Rubber band

Wire cutters
Chain-nose pliers
Wire drawplate
    (*Soft Flex Company*)
End caps
18-gauge copper or sterling
    silver wire

Clasp
Decorative cylinder beads that fit
    over finished chain
Liver of Sulfur or small butane
    torch (*optional*)

1. Measure off 1½ yards of 24-gauge wire, and wrap the wire around a credit card five wraps so that when you remove the card you have five loops to gather.

2. Wrap the end of the wire to bundle the loops at one end; spread out the loops at the other end, spacing them evenly. The wires will look like a broom.

3. Slip the wire bundle over the end of the dowel.

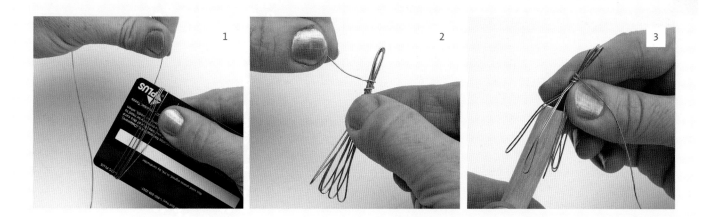

4. Use a rubber band to secure the bundle to the dowel. Adjust each loop so that the loops are evenly spaced around the dowel. This part is important, as it will affect the neatness of the chain later.

5. Thread the working end of the wire through the first loop, entering the loop from the right side.

6. Pull the wire to form a new loop as shown. Move to the next loop on the right to continue.

7. Thread the wire through each loop around the dowel, making sure your tension is even and consistent.

8. When you reach the first loop, bring the wire through the right side again, except instead of working the wire through the loop, bring it under the "neck" of the base of the previous loop as shown. Continue around the dowel, bringing the wire around the neck of each loop.

9. Continue this pattern for several rows; this is called a single-weave pattern (shown), or you could continue this pattern for the entire bracelet. For a dense pattern, switch to the double-weave pattern explained in the following steps after a few rows of the single-weave pattern.

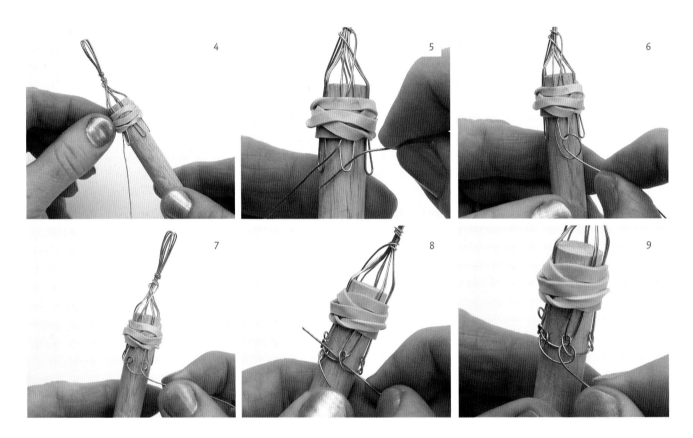

10. To form a double weave, bring the wire through the "neck" behind the loop of the second loop from the bottom. You will see two wires on each side of the loop as shown in the photo; if you look for the two wires on each side, this will help you easily locate where to insert the wire each time as you work around. This is the pattern you will follow to complete the rest of the chain.

11. To add a new piece of wire, cut off a new piece about 1 yard in length to work with. End the previous wire midloop without completing the loop. Leave the wire tail exiting at the top left and pointed up. Bring the new wire through where the old wire left off, with the tail of the

new wire sticking out on the right side. Bend both wire ends upward to keep them out of the way as you work.

12. Wrap the new wire down and complete the loop you would have formed with the old wire, continuing around as done in the previous rows. Leave the tails about ½ inch or longer; these will be clipped with wire cutters and worked into the chain later.

13. Continue adding wire to build the chain.

14. Slide the work up and off the dowel as you go. You can stop when the chain is about 5 inches long. It will lengthen about ⅓ inch after you pull it through the

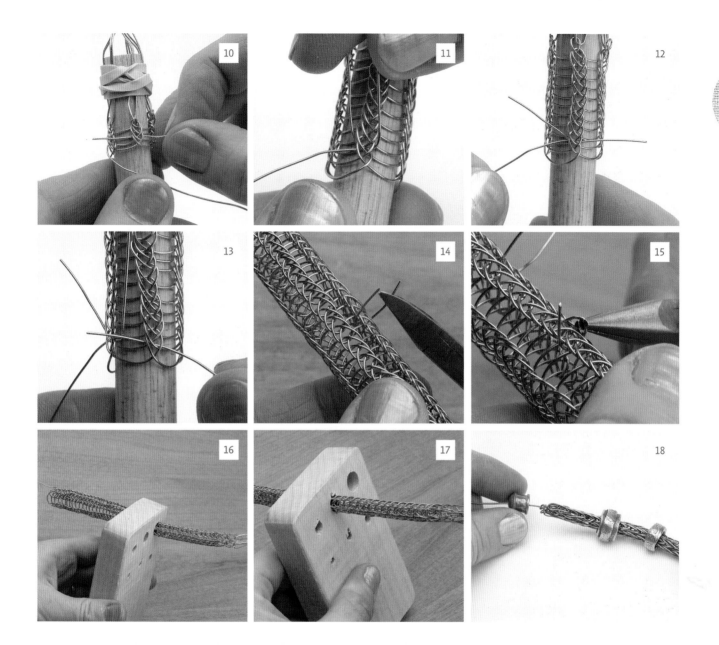

drawplate. When finished weaving, slide the chain off of the dowel. Cut all of the ends of the stray wires to about ¼ inch long.

15. Tuck the tails into the work with chain-nose pliers. The wires should be bent downward toward the end you finished with and positioned to blend in with the weave of the knitting.

16. To lengthen and compress the chain, pull the work through the largest hole on the drawplate, pulling from the end you started the work on.

17. Pull through progressively smaller holes until you

reach the desired width that fits your end caps. This example was pulled through three holes to reach the desired diameter.

18. For directions on adding the end caps and clasp to finish the bracelet, see steps 16–20 of the Spool Knit Wire Bracelet (pages 124–125). The decorative cylinder beads are added before adding the final end cap and clasp. If you would like to patina the piece, dip it in a solution of Liver of Sulfur until darkened (see directions on page 29). You can also use a small butane torch to patina copper. This helps if the copper is coated and is stubborn about taking a patina with Liver of Sulfur.

Braided Handkerchief and Ribbon Bracelet

On occasion, a grandmother or aunt would give me pretty printed handkerchiefs when they noticed my admiration of the design. The floral patterns are too beautiful to sit unused in a dusty old drawer. It's exciting to use them in an updated way. The delicate patterns and cotton fabric construction make them a perfect material for fabric jewelry design. Cotton handkerchiefs, ribbon yarn, and netted fibers were used to make this bracelet, but you can use fabric in place of the handkerchiefs. Tear cotton fabric strips with the grain of the fabric prior to braiding them. Combine ribbon or other types of fibers with the fabric to add texture to the bracelet, and add stones or beads to dress them up. Be creative by using fabric scraps and beads you already have on hand. You might be surprised at the range of possibilities when you combine unusual materials.

SUPPLIES

Cotton handkerchief	Round-nose pliers	Button
Scissors	Wire cutters	Sewing needle
Ribbon	Chain-nose pliers	Thread
24- or 22-gauge half-hard sterling silver wire, 9 inches in length	Clipboard	
	3 semiprecious stone beads	

1. Tear four 1-inch-wide strips from the handkerchief. Make a snip with the scissors to get started, and then tear the strips the entire length of the handkerchief. Cut two ribbons the same length as the handkerchief strips.

2. Gather the ends of two strips of the handkerchief and one ribbon to form one end of the bracelet. Using round-nose pliers, form a loop with the wire around the ends of the strips and ribbon about 1½ inches up from the bottom. Wrap the wire around the base of the loop a few times. Clip the end of the wire with wire cutters and use chain-nose pliers to tuck in the end of the wire as shown.

3. Clip the wire to a clipboard to hold the work in place as you braid. Bring the loose ends down and work them in as you braid. This photo shows how the ends are being braided in to hide and secure them.

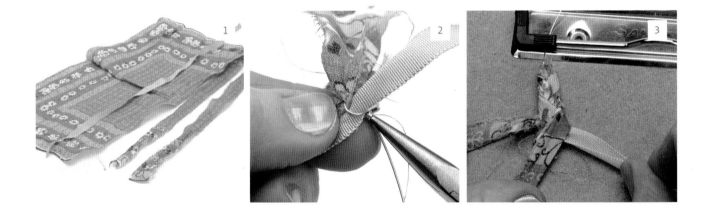

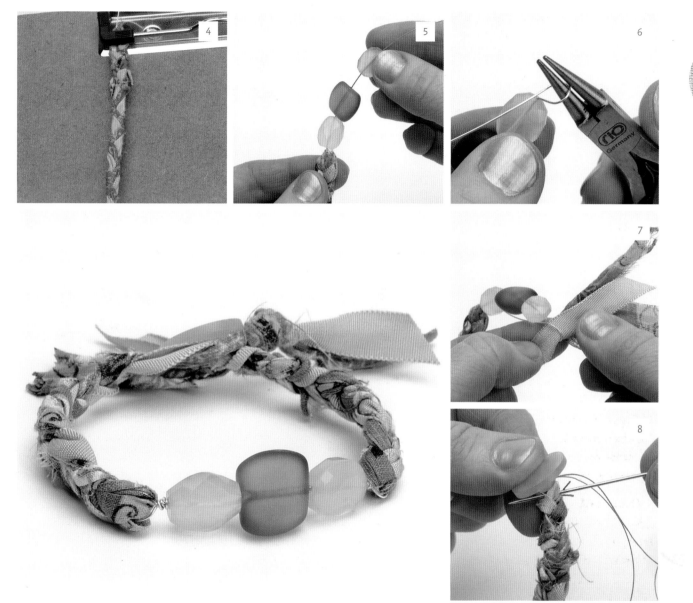

4. Continue braiding for about 5 inches.

5. Thread three beads onto the wire.

6. Form a wire loop at the end of the beads with round-nose pliers.

7. Add the other strips to form the other side of the bracelet. Wrap the end of the wire and clip off the excess as you did in step 2.

8. Braid the strips and ribbon as you did in step 4, working the ends into the braid to secure. To finish the bracelet, measure it to your wrist and make one side a little longer than the other for the closure. Loosen the braid at the end a bit so that the button will fit through the braid for the closure. To form the closure, knot the ends of each side of the braided work with an overhand knot (see directions on page 30-31). (For directions on this type of closure, see step 9 of the Resin Clay Flower Bracelet on page 79). Sew a button on the shorter side. Fasten the bracelet to your wrist by passing the button through the braided work near the knot.

Braided Macramé Ribbon Bracelet

I'm a habitual scrap collector of lace and trims, so this is the perfect project to recycle my favorite pieces and to convert them into pretty pieces of jewelry. I like to mix old with new and incorporate metal beads with large holes.

SUPPLIES

3 ribbons, each 1 yard in length
Clipboard
Beads with large holes

Short piece of wire or stiff string
Hill Tribe silver flower charm
Button

Sewing needle
Thread
Scissors

1. Gather the three ribbons together and tie them together with an overhand knot (see directions on pages 30–31) 12 inches from one end.

2. Secure the ribbons to a clipboard near the knot, leaving the 12 inches free at the top. You will be forming the middle section of the bracelet first. Start braiding the three ribbons, adding beads along the braid.

3. To thread the end of the ribbon through the bead, fold a short piece of wire in half over the end of the ribbon to form a makeshift needle and pull through the bead as shown.

4. Continue braiding and adding beads along the work for about 4 inches. This is the middle section of the bracelet, so you can vary how much of it you would like to braid. A series of square knots will be tied to finish each side of the bracelet until it fits your wrist.

5. With the braid still attached to the clipboard, bring one of the ribbons to the center (here it's the black ribbon). To begin the square knot (see directions pages 30-31), take a ribbon on the left and cross it over the middle ribbon as shown. It should look like a 4.

6. Bring the ribbon on the right over the tail of the other ribbon and pass it under both the center and the left ribbons as shown. Pull the ribbon through the open loop on the left.

7. Pull both the right and the left ribbon ends evenly to secure the knot around the middle ribbon.

8. Repeat steps 5–7 to make the second half of the square knot, except you will be starting with the ribbon on the right side to begin the knot as shown.

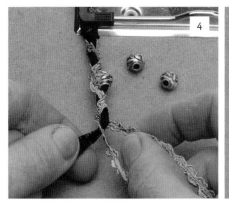

Hobbies

Inspiration WHAT'S COOKING?

When I'm stressed I make cookies. I've been baking since I was little and love to bake almost more than anything else. I have lots of cookbooks and files stuffed full of recipes that I clip from magazines—and will never have time to make. I love the challenge of finding a recipe for something I want to learn how to make; it's like a treasure hunt.

When I was a young teenager I learned to decorate cakes and make icing flowers. I use the same skills I learned from making the icing flowers to shape clay flowers for jewelry. After making a few too many cakes, I was done decorating with icing. Now I use all of the cake-decorating tools, cookie cutters, fondant shapers, rollers, and cookie molds for craft purposes. Cake-decorating stores are great places to find tools for jewelry making.

Candy making is also something I enjoy. Candy making is a lost art, and techniques for making real fondants and chocolates aren't widely known. I have cherished recipes that have been passed down from professional candy makers along with time-tested family favorites. During the holidays, my husband and I like to dip chocolates with various fillings to send to friends and relatives. We've come up with some interesting combinations over the years, although I'm not sure how well the hot chili chocolates were received. It's no surprise that people say my jewelry reminds them of candy. There's no doubt it has a big influence on my projects.

Sweet Treats Polymer Clay Charm Bracelet

Polymer clay is the perfect medium for making realistic mini cookies and pastries. Polymer clay has been used for dollhouse miniatures for many years to make food and accessories. These little pastries can be turned into charms by adding plastic-coated wire and attaching them to a chain. I copied some favorite cookbooks and reduced them to make miniature cookbook charms in addition to the pastries for the bracelet. The cookbooks belonged to my mother. I spent plenty of time in my younger years making some of the recipes found inside.

SUPPLIES

Polymer clay—light green, lime green, white, beige, black, light brown, red, and blue

Clay roller or pasta roller

Sharp tissue blade or mat cutter blade

Plastic-coated wire

Glass baking dish

Sculpey® gloss glaze

Brush

Small clay cutters or canapé cutters

Acrylic gloss paint and acrylic medium

Toothpick

Glitter (*optional*)

Reduced-size copy of paper cookbook cover

Scissors

Sobo white glue

Mod Podge decoupage medium (*Plaid Creative Group*)

Flat brush

Bracelet chain and clasp

2 chain-nose pliers

Jump rings

Acrylic paint

Liquitex acrylic modeling paste, medium or heavy gel medium (*Liquitex*)

Wire cutters

1. To make the fruit tart, use a clay roller or a pasta roller (if you have one specifically for polymer clay) to roll out a small sheet of beige or light brown clay to make the base and the crust. Cut out a circle of the clay for the base of the tart and a narrow strip of the clay for the edge of the crust.

2. Twist the strip to make a spiral of clay to go around the base. Press the strip around the circle base, cutting and joining the ends to complete the twisted rope around the circle. Press the clay to adhere.

3. To make the kiwi fruit, you will use light green and lime green clay. Black clay is used for the seeds. The fruit

1   2   3

will be created by forming a cane of clay to slice in cross sections. Roll out a log of black clay, wrap a sheet of light green clay around the black clay, and join the seam. Roll the wrapped log of clay until it becomes longer and thinner. Using a sharp tissue blade or a mat cutter blade, cut the log into several cross sections, which will form the seeds for the fruit.

4. Roll out a log of light green clay, and place the black and green sections around the log as shown until you

completely surround the center. Roll this bundle down to compact the clay a bit.

5. Wrap this log with a sheet of lime green clay. Roll this down until the log, or rope, of clay is about ¼ inch thick. Let the cane rest for a while.

6. To make the kiwi fruits, use a sharp tissue blade or a mat cutter blade to cut off slices of clay.

7. Make small round balls of red and blue clay to make berries for the tart. Press the berries and kiwi slices into the base of the clay tart. Cut a piece of wire with wire cutters to make a twisted loop and insert it into the top of the tart for hanging. Bake the piece on a glass baking dish at 275 degrees Fahrenheit for 30 minutes. Cool.

8. To glaze the pie, after it's baked, brush on a layer of Sculpey gloss glaze and let the glaze dry.

9. To make cake charms, use small clay cutters or canapé cutters to cut heart, square, or round cake shapes out of a thick pad of beige clay. Insert a wire hook in the top for hanging the charms. Bake the pieces on a glass baking dish at 275 degrees Fahrenheit for 30 minutes. Note: Be sure to follow manufacturer's safety warnings and avoid burning the clay. Cool.

10. To make frosting for the cakes, mix acrylic paint with acrylic paste or gel medium to thicken the paint. Use a toothpick to apply the paint to frost the cake.

11. As an option: Add a baked clay berry and leaf to the clay when the paint is wet or sprinkle glitter on the paint before it dries so it looks like granulated sugar.

12. To make cookies, roll out a sheet of beige or light brown clay about $1/16$ inch thick and cut out cookie shapes with small cutters. Insert a twisted wire hook for hanging, and bake the pieces on a glass baking dish at 275 degrees Fahrenheit for 30 minutes. Cool. To ice the cookies, use an acrylic gloss paint to cover the surface.

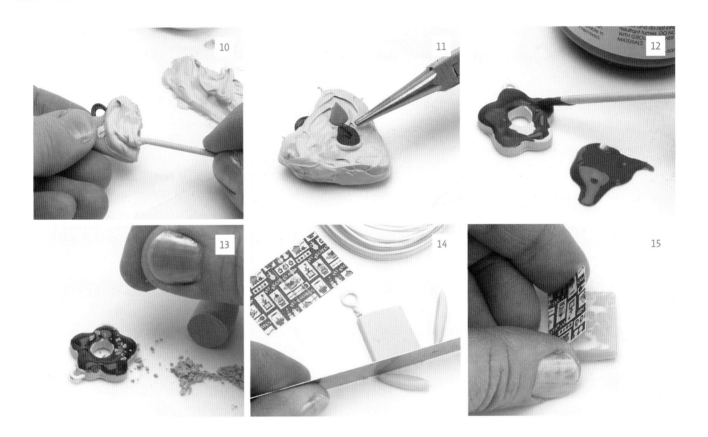

13. Decorate with glitter or "nuts." The nuts are made by baking a piece of beige clay on a glass baking dish at 275 degrees Fahrenheit for 30 minutes. Cool and then chop the clay up finely with a blade. Sprinkle the clay nuts over the wet paint. Let the paint dry well.

14. To make mini cookbooks, scan or photocopy the cover of your favorite cookbook. Reduce the image on a computer to about 1 inch in height, using a photo-editing computer software program such as Photoshop. Cut the image from the paper and roll out a thick sheet of beige clay, cutting it to fit the inside of the cookbook image.

Insert a twisted wire hook and bake the piece on a glass baking dish at 275 degrees Fahrenheit for 30 minutes. Cool.

15. Use Sobo white glue to glue the cover of the book around the baked clay to form the cookbook. After the glue dries, apply the decoupage glue to the surface with a brush to protect the cover. To assemble the bracelet, use chain-nose pliers to attach the charms to a bracelet chain with jump rings.

Metal Clay Cookie Mold Pendant

Springerle cookie molds were originally carved from wood with ornate designs. They can also be made of clay or metal. Some of the earliest molds came from Switzerland and were used to tell a story at a time when many people couldn't read. The molds portray holidays, family life, animals, flowers, seasons, and religious scenes. The molds were used to emboss designs onto dough that was then baked into traditional anise-flavored cookies, which originated in Germany. Reproductions of these antique molds are made of a resin/wood composite, which makes them accessible and affordable.

I have a particular fondness for these molds because my ancestors come from both Switzerland and Germany. Many of their baking traditions have been passed down through my family, including recipes for molded cookies. Springerle molds make beautiful cookies, but I also like using them for texturing clay. You can find the molds online or in specialty baking stores.

SUPPLIES

Springerle cookie molds
    (*House on the Hill*)
Olive oil
Small brush
PMC3 silver metal clay
Roller (*optional*)
X-Acto knife

Needle tool or other hole-forming
    tool
Mug warmer (*optional*)
Nail file
Paintbrush
Water
Firebrick or solderite pad

Burnishing tool
Purchased chain
Jump ring
2 chain-nose pliers
Bead dangle (*optional*)
Small butane torch
Brass burnishing brush

1. Brush a small amount of olive oil on the mold to prevent sticking.

2. Pinch off a small ball of clay to use for the charm. Press the clay onto the mold. Flatten the back with the roller or your fingers.

3. Remove the clay from the mold.

4. Cut out the shape with the knife.

5. Form a hole in the top of the charm with the needle tool. This will be refined later, so don't worry if it's not large or perfect enough. You only need a pilot hole at this stage. You can let the clay dry on a mug warmer to speed the process.

6. If using a mug warmer, your charm should be ready to refine in about 1 hour. Be careful at this stage, as the clay is very fragile in the greenware state (dry clay that isn't fired). Use the tip of the knife to enlarge and refine the hole, spinning it all the way around as though you were drilling. Don't apply pressure; let the knife shave the hole as you twirl it around. Make sure you don't get too close to the edge of the clay. Work to enlarge the hole through the back of the piece, too.

7. Use a nail file to refine the edges. Sand around the edges and soften the point by rounding it out with the file. Smooth any imperfections with a small paintbrush and water. Let the piece dry thoroughly before firing, preferably overnight. The piece should be bone dry. To fire the piece, place it on a fireproof brick or solderite pad (see directions on page 28). Alternately, you can fire the charms in a kiln at 1650 degrees Fahrenheit for 5 minutes.

8. The piece will appear white after firing. Burnishing it will bring out the silver reflection. Use a soft brass scratch brush to burnish the piece.

9. Burnish the piece using a burnishing tool over the high spots to bring out the sparkle of the silver.

10. Use chain-nose pliers to add a jump ring to the charm. Close the ring after attaching the charm to the chain. Add a bead dangle for an accent if desired. As an option, you can add a patina to the charm (see directions on page 29).

der
bak
plac
with

Cut
greased
Meanw
into qu
and cho
togethe
roll and
several
cracker
nish eac
Marasch

SWEETS

ST. JOHNS
THEATRE
PORTLAND, OREGON
EST. PR. 55c
FED. TAX 5c
TOTAL 60c
024333

ST. JOHNS
THEATRE
PORTLAND, OREGON
EST. PR. 55c
FED. TAX 5c
TOTAL 60c
024332

GLOBE TICKET CO. OF WASH., TACOMA

GLOBE TICKET CO. OF WASH., TACOMA

sará oro materia del mio

O buono apo l'último

fami del fatto

amal

Inspiration GARDENING BOTANICALS

My mother's favorite hobby was gardening. She spent hours designing her garden and studying the various varieties of plants that were native to our Northwest region. She was originally from Idaho, where the soil and seasonal temperatures were very different from the Northwest, so growing native plants became an interest of hers. There were stacks of gardening magazines and seed catalogs around our house that she would save for inspiration and for ordering bulbs and perennials. Each spring she would fill large planters with her own carefully selected arrangements of flowers to add beauty to our back porch. Common favorites for the pots included fuchsias, geraniums, and impatiens, which all grew very well in the climate. Our surrounding garden consisted of azaleas, rhododendrons, hydrangeas, dogwoods, and roses.

After I had my own home and garden in Utah, my mom taught me which plants would do well in my climate zone, with its harsh winters and hot summers. I learned the names of perennials and how to grow them successfully. She taught me landscaping design and where to place the plants based on the exposure to the sun. I find it difficult to find the time it takes to keep up a beautiful garden, but I enjoy what time I do spend outdoors. Planting and watching flowers bloom in spring, summer, and early fall is very satisfying. Flowers and plant life are probably number one for me as far as a jewelry inspiration. I have to work hard not to make everything into a flower.

Etched Copper Botanical Bracelet

This etching process uses electricity to safely etch metal using copper sulfate, an environmentally friendly solution. Unlike other popular etching materials that must be disposed of as hazardous waste, copper sulfate can be recycled or eventually washed down the drain. My husband, Dan, is an electrical engineer, and he designed an electronic controller that is programmed to adjust the power to evenly etch the metal that is submerged in a solution of copper sulfate.

Because copper sulfate solution doesn't absorb the copper (the copper plates bottom of the working pan), you can save the solution and use it over and over. After applying a design onto the metal, the solution and the controller does the rest and you are left with a beautiful etched image.

A laser copy was used to create a resist for the designs described in this project. This is just one simple way to apply a resist. Other resists such as PnP Blue or UV film can be used in place of laser transfers. Designs to transfer can be found from clip art sources or you can draw your own designs using an oil based paint pen. I like to use illustrations that remind me of walks in the woods, with lots of fern and thistly patterns, which make lovely jewelry designs.

SUPPLIES

Black-and-white toner-based design image
E3 Etch® Paper (*Sherri Haab Designs*)
Scissors
Copper blanks
600 grit sandpaper
Rubbing alcohol
Cotton swabs
Wooden board for ironing
Household iron
Press cloth (*old pillowcase works well*)
Dish

Towel or clean cloth
Oil-based paint marker or fingernail polish, any color that lets you see where you are painting it
Heavy packing tape
E3 Etch® kit (*Sherri Haab Designs*)
Disposable plastic teaspoon
Acetone or acetone-based fingernail polish remover
Metal punch tool (*Burnt Offerings*)
4 eyelets, size ³/₃₂ (*Burnt Offerings*)
Small metal file
Eyelet-setting tool (*Burnt Offerings*)

Hammer
Mallet (*Burnt Offerings*)
Metal block or anvil
Black Max
Pro-Polish Polishing Pad (*Rio Grande*)
1.5mm leather cord, 1 yard
2 large jump rings
2 chain-nose pliers
2 pieces of 26- or 28-gauge copper wire, each 12 inches in length
Wire cutters
Lobster clasp

1. The following instructions are for how to use the direct toner transfer method. Print a black-and-white design image into E3 Etch Paper using a toner-based laser copier. This design will be heat transferred onto the metal. Choose a design with strong lines and crisp details. The black areas of the design will act as a resist. Etching will occur wherever copper is exposed, creating a recessed pattern. Cut the design to fit your copper blank. If the image has text, print the image in reverse, or as a mirror image, so the orientation of the text will appear correctly on the copper. Prepare the copper blank by sanding it with sandpaper. This will give the metal some "tooth" to help the design to adhere.

2. Clean the surface of the copper blank with rubbing alcohol using a cotton swab. Dry the piece, and avoid touching the surface.

3. To transfer the image to the copper blank, place the

blank on a wooden board and place the image facedown on the side of the copper you cleaned in step 2.

4. Cover the paper with a press cloth. Being careful not to displace the paper as you iron, press the piece with an iron set on a high heat (cotton or linen setting); press with firm pressure, putting your weight into it for about 2 minutes. Check the piece to make sure the paper has adhered. If pressed properly, the paper should be flat with no ripples. You can press longer to make sure it's properly heated for the transfer.

5. After the piece cools for a few minutes, place the piece in a dish of water and let it soak for about 10 minutes. Carefully remove the paper backing by rolling the paper

fibers off with your fingers. Re-dip the piece in water to moisten if needed. Dry off the piece with a towel or cloth. Don't worry if white paper fibers remain. They won't interfere with the etching process.

6. If sections of the design didn't transfer, use an oil-based paint marker to color in those areas. Alternately, nail polish also works in place of the pen as a resist. If your transfer didn't work, you can always sand the piece and start again.

7. To prepare your copper for etching, paint around the edges of the piece with the oil-based paint marker or fingernail polish, and place a piece of heavy packing tape over to mask off half of the back side as shown. The other

half of the copper is left exposed to allow you to add the electrode wire described in the next step.

8. Bend an aluminum wire (included in the kit) into a 90-degree angle, or L shape, at about the middle of the wire. This wire will serve as an electrode to conduct the electricity. Make a few short zigzag, or S-shaped, bends at the end of the wire. Position the zigzag end onto the exposed part of the copper. The metals must touch to properly conduct electricity. Place a second piece of tape

over the wire to hold it in place and protect the copper from the etching solution. Fold the edges of the tape over to reinforce them. Leave a little tape exposed around the edges, as this extra tape is helpful in step 10.

9. Before etching, read the safety instructions included with the etching kit. Keep the supplies away from children and pets, as it's hazardous to ingest. To etch the piece, mix and dissolve four heaping teaspoons of the granular copper sulfate powder in 12 ounces of water

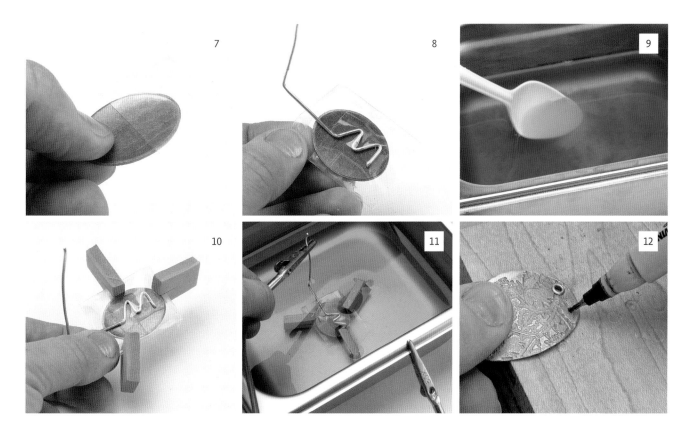

in the stainless pan (powder and pan included in kit). If you have hard water you will need to use distilled water, as crystals will form in hard water, and this can interfere with the etching process. Warm water helps the crystals to dissolve faster.

10. Attach the foam spacers (included in the kit) over the taped edges. Avoid covering your design with the spacers, as it will interfere with the etching process.

11. Attach the black clip to the pan and the red clip to the aluminum wire. Set the piece down on the bottom of the pan with the spacers touching the bottom. The spacers will keep the copper level and close to the bottom without touching. If the piece is small and attempts to

float, cover the pan and cables with a dishcloth. Now plug in the controller and set on "fast." It will take 2 hours for the etching to occur. For a deeper etch you can leave it for an extra hour or longer. Stop etching when the desired depth is obtained.

12. Rinse off the piece and dry it after etching. Remove the ink with acetone or acetone-based fingernail polish remover using a cotton swab. Mark hole placements on each side of the copper piece with the oil-based paint marker. You can mark one hole in the center or a hole on each side, depending on how you would like to hang the finished pendant.

13. Use a metal punch to make holes on the sides of the piece for the eyelets. This punch tightens down and punches a hole in the metal. It has two hole sizes. Use the side that corresponds with the eyelet. The eyelet should fit tightly in the hole.

14. Place the eyelet through the hole.

15. Use a metal file to file the height of the eyelet that is exposed until it measures about half the diameter of the hole. For example, if the hole is 2mm in diameter, file the part of the eyelet that is exposed until it's about 1mm in height.

16. Use the eyelet setter to hammer the eyelet in place (see photo). After setting the eyelets, you may want the entire piece to have a soft curve; use a mallet to hammer the piece over a curved form or bracelet mandrel (not shown).

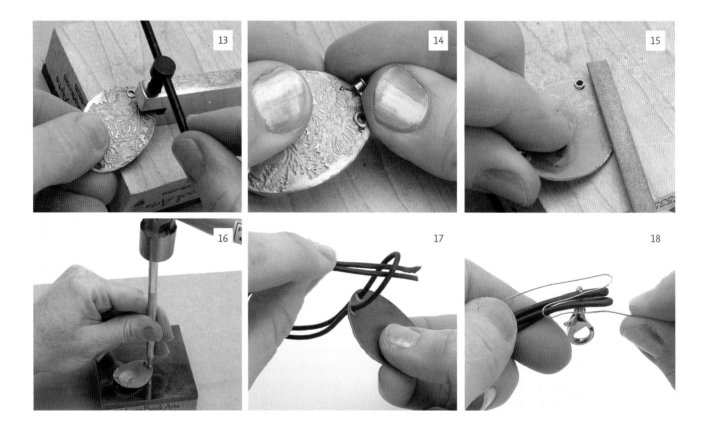

17. To patina the piece, use a cotton swab to add the patina (see directions on page 29). Wipe away the raised areas of the copper with a polishing pad. To attach the leather cord, cut an 18-inch piece of cord, make a loop with it, and thread the ends of the cord through the eyelets on one side to make a lark's head knot as shown (see directions on page 30-31). Repeat on the other side.

18. Fit the bracelet to your wrist and adjust the cord to fit where the clasp will be placed. Slide a jump ring over the cords and fold the ends over with chain-nose pliers to secure with wire. To make a wire wrap to finish the ends, make a Z shape with the end of the copper wire and hold the end parallel to the cords.

19. Begin wrapping the wire tightly a few times around the cords and the Z-shaped wire, wrapping from left to right.

20. Continue wrapping the wire tightly around the cords as shown.

21. Using the chain-nose pliers, untwist the loop on the left to keep it from kinking as you cinch up the wrap.

22. Bring the end of the wire through the loop on the right as shown.

23. Tighten the wire wrap by pulling the loop on the right side to cinch the wire loop on the left.

24. Pull the wire on the left side tight to close up the loop on the right side. Pull tightly until the loop disappears under the wire wrapping. Clip off the ends of the wire with wire cutters for a neat finish. Trim off the ends of the cord close to the wrapped wire. Repeat on the other side to include a clasp attached to the jump ring to finish.

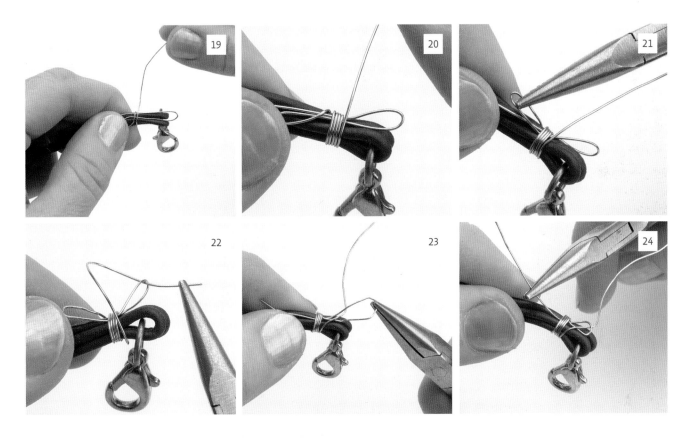

Metal Clay Molded Bee Pendant

I live in Utah, which is known as the Beehive State. Although I grew up in the Northwest, my husband and I moved to Utah shortly after we married. I have deep roots in the Beehive State, as many of my maternal ancestors were among the Mormon pioneers who braved harsh conditions in the mid 1800s to settle in the Rocky Mountains. These early pioneers were known for their perseverance and hard work. The honeybee represented the industry and cooperation of the people and became the state's symbol.

Bees are beautiful and complex creatures, and I love old illustrations of bees and beehives. I find hundreds of bees humming around the flowers in my herb garden each spring and summer, especially around the sage. Bees are a popular theme in the jewelry I make. In my workshops I've seen that students also find bee themes appealing. When I bring the bee molds to class, I find that my students eagerly wait their turn as the molds are being passed around for each person to make his or her own little bee charm or bee-themed piece of jewelry.

SUPPLIES

2-part silicone mold putty or polymer clay, talc powder, and olive oil
Brass stamping or button of bee
PMC3 silver clay
X-ACTO knife
Needle tool
Mug warmer
Nail file

Small paintbrush
Water
Small butane torch
Firebrick or solderite pad
Brass burnishing brush
Burnishing tool
Liver of Sulfur
Pro-Polish Polishing Pads
   (*Rio Grande*)

Charm
2 eye pin wires
Chain-nose pliers
Round-nose pliers
Chain and clasp
Decorative beads
1 head pin
Wire cutters

1. Make a silicone putty mold (see directions on page 26). Press a stamping or button into the putty. This mold was made with a brass button of a bee.

2. After the mold is cured, remove the bee button.

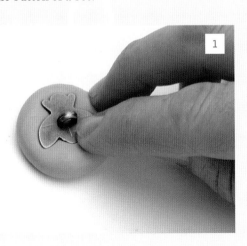

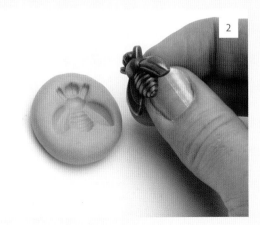

3. Unwrap the silver clay and pinch off a small amount to press into the mold. Press the clay and roll over the back to flatten. Remove the clay from the mold.

4. Alternatively, you can use polymer clay instead of silicone mold putty to make a mold. However, you must use talc powder as a release agent to keep the clay from sticking while pressing the button in the clay before baking the clay. After baking the polymer clay, use olive oil as a release agent for the metal clay. This photo shows the baked polymer mold and the removal of the metal clay from the mold.

5. After removing the metal clay from the mold, cut around the clay to make a shape, or leave the clay rough around the edges for an organic look. Use a needle tool to form a hole on each side at the top for attaching the pieces of chain and one at the bottom for hanging a bead dangle. These are just pilot holes; you will refine the holes and enlarge them later when the clay is dry.

6. Let the clay dry. You can speed this up by placing the piece on a mug warmer. Refine the edges with a nail file; be careful, as the piece is fragile at this stage.

7. Use the tip of an X-Acto knife to enlarge the hole. Spin the knife all the way around as though you were drilling the hole. Don't apply pressure; let the knife shave the hole as you twirl it around. Make sure you don't get too close to the edge of the clay or you may break through.

8. Smooth any imperfections with a small paintbrush and water. Let the piece dry thoroughly before firing. To fire the piece place it on a fireproof brick or solderite pad (see directions on page 28). Alternately, you can fire the charms in a kiln at 1650 degrees Fahrenheit for 5 minutes.

9. The piece will appear white after firing. Burnishing it will bring out the silver reflection. Use a soft brass burnishing brush to burnish the piece.

10. Use a burnishing tool to burnish the metal further, which will make the high areas sparkle with shine.

11. To add a patina, dip the piece in a solution of Liver of Sulfur or other type of patina (see directions on page 29). Attach a charm to an eye pin wire using chain-nose pliers. Form a wrapped loop (see directions on page 23) with chain-nose pliers to attach the eye pin wire to the chain. A decorative bead was added to the wire before attaching the charm. Repeat the same step on the other side.

12. Attach a head pin with beads to the bottom of the charm using chain-nose pliers. Wrap the wire at the base of the loop and clip off the excess wire with wire cutters to finish.

13. Use chain-nose pliers to attach a clasp to the ends of the chain to complete the necklace.

9

10

11

12

13

Contributors

Cheryl Tempest Burton
Jewelry designer, heirloom photo bezels
e-mail: ctempestburton@msn.com

Julie Collings
Craft designer, inspiration boards
blog: theadventuresofbluegirlxo.
blogspot.com

Marina Collings
Illustrator, Rock 'n' Roll Shrink
Art Necklaces
e-mail: marinacollings@gmail.com

Tracy Stanley
Viking Knit Wire Bracelet
website: www.wiredarts.net
e-mail: tracy@wiredarts.net

Resources

Actíva Products, Inc.
www.activaproducts.com
Recycled papier-mâché clay

Alumilite Corporation
www.alumilite.com
Resin, 2-part silicone mold putty

Aves Studio
www.avesstudio.com
Apoxie Sculpt 2-part epoxy resin clay

Bedrock Industries
www.bedrockindustries.com
Mechanically tumbled glass

Burnt Offerings
www.burntofferings.com
Tin and metal tools, eyelets, metal punches,
steel blocks, hammers

Creative Paperclay
www.paperclay.com
Air-hardening modeling material

Fire Mountain Gems and Beads
www.firemountaingems.com
Beads, jewelry findings and supplies, Ferido
2-part epoxy resin clay

FISKARS
www.fiskarscrafts.com
Craft hand crill

G-S Supplies
www.gssupplies.com
G-S Hypo Cement, G-S Hypo Fabric
Cement

House on the Hill, Inc.
www.houseonthehill.net
Springerle molds, baking supplies

Jane's Fiber and Beads
www.janesfiberandbeads.com
C-Lon bead cord, beading supplies

Liquitex
www.liquitex.com
Acylic paint, gel mediums, sculpting paste

Metal Clay Findings
www.metalclayfindings.com
Fine silver findings, metal clay

Metal Clay Supply
www.metalclaysupply.com
PMC, Art Clay Silver, bronzclay, tools and
supplies

Moondance Designs
www.moondancedesigns.com
C-Lon bead cord, beads, kits

Plaid Creative Group
www.plaidonline.com
Mod Podge decoupage medium

My ELEMENTS
www.myelementsbyyvonne.com
Baked enamel chain, jewelry kits

Objects and Elements
www.objectsandelements.com
Bezels, resin, metal, wire, jewelry supplies,
ICE Resin

Polyform Products Co.
www.sculpey.com
Premo! Sculpey polymer clay

Rio Grande
www.riogrande.com
Jewelry supplies, wire, pliers, patina
solutions, 3M polishing paper, Pro-Polish

Polishing Pads, PMC, bronzclay, 2-part
silicone mold putty

Sherri Haab Designs
www.sherrihaab.com
ITS, resin, Pearl Ex Powered Pigments,
molds, bezels, ring blanks, books, DVDs,
kits

Shrinky Dinks
www.shrinkydinks.com
Shrink plastic

Silver Creek Leather Co.
www.silvercreekleather.com
Leather cord, suede, hardware and supplies

Smooth-On, Inc.
www.smooth-on.com
Resin, mold-making supplies, casting
supplies, 2-part silicone mold putty

Soft Flex Company
www.softflexcompany.com
Knitting spools, wire drawplate, wire

Tandy Leather Factory
www.tandyleatherfactory.com
Leather stamping tools and supplies

TAP Plastics, Inc.
www.tapplastics.com
Clear cabochons, resin, casting and
sculpting supplies

The Bouncing Bead
www.thebouncingbead.com
Beads, Swarovski crystals, jewelry-making
supplies

Thunderbird Supply Company
www.thunderbirdsupply.com
Beads, findings, wire

Tinsel Trading Company
www.tinseltrading.com
Metal threads, vintage flowers and leaves,
trims, ribbons

Toner Crafts
www.tonercrafts.com
Weave Wheel, Fun Wire

Volcano Arts
www.volcanoarts.biz
Metalsmithing tools and supplies, steel
block, eyelets, bookbinding supplies

West Coast Sea Glass
www.westcoastseaglass.com
Genuine sea glass

Whole Lotta Whimsy
www.wholelottawhimsy.com
Metal clay, polymer clay, resin, books,
DVDs

Wired Arts
www.wiredarts.net
Tracy Stanley: tracy@wiredarts.net
Jewelry kits, Viking Knit Wire Bracelet kit,
classes

Index

Acorn Charms, Polymer Clay, 64–67
Antique Button Pendants, 86–88
Baking-inspired jewelry
    about: inspirations for, 137
    Metal Clay Cookie Mold Pendant, 142,
      143–145
    Sweet Treats Polymer Clay Charm Bracelet,
      138, 139–141
Bead, button, and charm jewelry. See also
    Bracelets and charms
    about: inspirations for, 85; making beads, 115;
      vintage glass and bead earrings, 92
    Antique Button Pendants, 86–88
    Briolette Stone Earrings with Bead Accents,
      96–97
    Cascading Violet Crystal and Pearl Earrings,
      94–95
    Cracker Jack Charm Bracelet, 100–103
    Lucite Flower Bracelets, 89–91
    Wrapped-Wire Briolette Bead Earrings, 98–99
Black Max, 29
Bracelets and charms
    Braided Handkerchief and Ribbon Bracelet,
      130–131
    Braided Macramé Ribbon Bracelet, 132–133
    Cracker Jack Charm Bracelet, 100–103
    Etched Copper Botanical Bracelet, 148,
      149–153
    Lucite Flower Bracelets, 89–91
    Monogram and Silhouette Brass Charm
      Bracelet, 49–51
    Polymer Clay Acorn Charms, 64–67
    Resin Clay Flower Bracelets, 76–79
    Spool Knit Wire Bracelet, 120, 121–125
    Stick-Woven Fiber Bracelet, 116, 117–119
    Sweet Treats Polymer Clay Charm Bracelet,
      138, 139–141
    Viking Knit Wire Bracelet, 126, 127–129
    Winter Solstice Charm Exchange Bracelet,
      68, 69–71
Braid, 30, 31
Braided Handkerchief and Ribbon Bracelet,
    130–131
Braided Macramé Ribbon Bracelet, 132–133
Briolette Stone Earrings with Bead Accents,
    96–97
Butane torch
    creating patina, 29
    firing metal clay, 28
Cascading Violet Crystal and Pearl Earrings,
    94–95
Charms. See Bracelets and charms
Classes, taking/teaching, 21
Cracker Jack Charm Bracelet, 100–103
Creative life, of author, 9–11
Creativity and inspiration. See also specific
    jewelry themes
    clipping, collecting, filing craft ideas, 19–20
    developing, 15–21
    idea notebooks for, 20
    organized chaos and, 16–19
    studio or workspace and, 16
    taking/teaching classes for, 21
Creepy Creature Papier-Mâché Pins, 56–57

Earrings
    Briolette Stone Earrings with Bead Accents,
      96–97
    Cascading Violet Crystal and Pearl Earrings,
      94–95
    Wrapped-Wire Briolette Bead Earrings, 98–99
Epoxy resin clay, mixing, 24
Etched Copper Botanical Bracelet, 148, 149–153
Eye pins, 24
Fairy-tail-inspired jewelry
    about: inspirations for, 75
    Fairy-Tale Bubble Necklace, 80–83
Fall-inspired jewelry
    about: inspirations for, 63
    Polymer Clay Acorn Charms, 64–67
Family heirloom jewelry
    about: inspirations for, 45
    Keepsake Photo Necklace, 46, 47–48
    Monogram and Silhouette Brass Charm
      Bracelet, 49–51
Fiber jewelry
    about: inspirations for, 115
    Braided Handkerchief and Ribbon Bracelet,
      130–131
    Braided Macramé Ribbon Bracelet, 132–133
    Spool Knit Wire Bracelet, 120, 121–125
    Stick-Woven Fiber Bracelet, 116, 117–119
    Viking Knit Wire Bracelet, 126, 127–129
Firing metal clay, 28
Flower jewelry
    about: inspirations for, 75
    Lucite Flower Bracelets, 89–91
    Resin Clay Flower Bracelets, 76–79
    Food jewelry. See Baking-inspired jewelry
Gardening botanicals
    about: inspirations for, 147
    Etched Copper Botanical Bracelet, 148,
      149–153
    Metal Clay Molded Bee Pendant, 154,
      155–157
Halloween jewelry. See Seasonal jewelry
Head pins, 24
Heart Pendants, Resin, 111–113
Ideas, developing. See Creativity and inspiration
Image transfers, 25
Inspiration. See Creativity and inspiration;
specific jewelry themes
Jewelry-making techniques, 22–31
    firing metal clay, 28
    head pins and eye pins, 24
    image transfers, 25
    jump rings, 23
    knots, 30–31
    mixing epoxy resin clay, 24
    mixing resin, 26–27
    patinas for metal, 29
    2-part silicone mold putty, 26
    wireworking, 22–24
    wrapped-wire loop, 23
Jump rings, 23
Keepsake Photo Necklace, 46, 47–48
Knots, 30–31
Lark's head knot, 30, 31
Liver of Sulfur, 29
Loop, wrapped-wire, 23. See also Eye pins
Lucite Flower Bracelets, 89–91
Metal Clay Cookie Mold Pendant, 142, 143–145
Metal clay, firing, 28
Metal Clay Molded Bee Pendant, 154, 155–157

Monogram and Silhouette Brass Charm Bracelet,
    49–51
Necklaces. See also Pendants
    Fairy-Tale Bubble Necklace, 80–83
    Halloween Button Necklace, 58, 59–61
    Keepsake Photo Necklace, 46, 47–48
    Pacific Ocean Beaded Necklace, 38, 39–41
    Rock 'n' Roll Shrink Art Necklaces, 108–110
Overhand knot, 30, 31
Pacific Ocean Beaded Necklace, 38, 39–41
Patinas for metal, 29
Pendants
    Antique Button Pendants, 86–88
    Metal Clay Cookie Mold Pendant, 142,
      143–145
    Metal Clay Molded Bee Pendant, 154,
      155–157
    Resin Heart Pendants, 111–113
    Sea Glass Image Pendants, 42–43
Pins, Creepy Creature Papier-Mâché, 56–57
Plastic jewelry
    about: history and inspirations, 107
    Resin Heart Pendants, 111–113
    Rock 'n' Roll Shrink Art Necklaces, 108–110
Pliers, 22, 23
Polymer Clay Acorn Charms, 64–67
Resin, 26–27
Resin Heart Pendants, 111–113
Resources, 158–159
Rings, Sea Urchin, 36–37
Rock 'n' Roll Shrink Art Necklaces, 108–110
Sea-inspired jewelry
    about: inspirations for, 35
    Pacific Ocean Beaded Necklace, 38, 39–41
    Sea Glass Image Pendants, 42–43
    Sea Urchin Rings, 36–37
Seasonal jewelry
    about: inspirations for, 55, 61, 63
    Creepy Creature Papier-Mâché Pins, 56–57
    Halloween Button Necklace, 58, 59–61
    Polymer Clay Acorn Charms, 64–67
    Winter Solstice Charm Exchange Bracelet, 68,
      69–71
Silhouette, making, 50
Silicone mold putty, 2-part, 26
Spool Knit Wire Bracelet, 120, 121–125
Square knot, 30, 31
Stick-Woven Fiber Bracelet, 116, 117–119
Studio, 16
Sweet Treats Polymer Clay Charm Bracelet, 138,
    139–141
Techniques. See Jewelry-making techniques
Tools and supplies, 22–23. See also specific projects
2-part Silicone mold putty, 26
Viking Knit Wire Bracelet, 126, 127–129
Winter-inspired jewelry, 68, 69–71
    about: inspirations for, 63
    Winter Solstice Charm Exchange Bracelet, 68,
      69–71
Wire cutters, 22
Wireworking, 22–24
    head pins and eye pins, 24
    jump rings, 23
    tools and supplies, 22–23
    wrapped-wire loop, 23
Workspace, 16
Woven jewelry. See Fiber jewelry
Wrapped-Wire Briolette Bead Earrings, 98–99
Wrapped-wire loop, 23